Editor

Erica N. Russikoff, M.A.

Illustrator

Clint McKnight

Cover Artist

Brenda DiAntonis

Editor in Chief

Ina Massler Levin, M.A.

Creative Director

Karen J. Goldfluss, M.S. Ed.

Art Coordinator

Renée Christine Yates

Imaging

Craig Gunnell

Publisher

Mary D. Smith, M.S. Ed.

Differential Nonfiction Reading

GRADE 4

Includes Standards & Benchmarks

- Each passage is written at 3 different levels: easier, average, more challenging
- Content areas include Science, Geography, History, and Language Arts

Author

Debra J. Housel, M.S. Ed.

Teacher Created Resources, Inc.

6421 Industry Way

Westminster, CA 92683

www.teachercreated.com

ISBN: 978-1-4206-2921-7

© 2010 Teacher Created Resources, Inc.

Reprinted, 2011

Made in U.S.A.

Table of Contents

Introduction

If you are like most teachers, your classroom includes a wide variety of students: average students, English language learners, gifted students, and learning disabled students. You may be expected to get your diverse student population, including special education students and those for whom English is a second language, to master grade-level, content-area material. That's a challenging task and one that requires grade-level, content-area materials written at several levels. *Differentiated Nonfiction Reading* was written specifically to help you respond to the demands of your state and local standards while meeting the needs of your students.

Purpose of This Book

Each passage in *Differentiated Nonfiction Reading* covers a grade-level appropriate curriculum topic in science, geography, history, or language arts. The Mid-continent Research for Education and Learning (McREL) standard and benchmark related to each passage is listed on pages 9–12.

Each content-area passage is written at three different levels: easy (below grade level), average (at grade level), and challenging (above grade level). After each passage is a set of comprehension questions that all of your students will answer. This enables your students to access the text and concepts at their instructional—rather than frustration—level, while requiring them to meet objective standards, just as they must do on standardized assessments.

Prepare Your Students to Read Content-Area Text

You can prepare your students to read the passages in *Differentiated Nonfiction Reading* by daily reading aloud a short nonfiction selection from another source. Reading content-area text aloud is critical to developing your students' ability to read it themselves.

Discussing content-area concepts with your class is also very important. Remember, however, that discussion can never replace reading aloud since people do not speak using the vocabulary and complex sentence structures of written language.

Readability

All of the passages in *Differentiated Nonfiction Reading* have a reading level that has been calculated by the Flesch-Kincaid Readability Formula. This formula, built into Microsoft Word®, determines a text's readability by calculating the number of words, syllables, and sentences.

Each passage is presented at three levels: easy, average, and challenging. *Easy* is below fourth-grade level; *average* is at fourth-grade level; and *challenging* is above fourth-grade level. The chart on page 13 shows you the specific reading levels of every passage.

To ensure that only you know the reading level at which each student is working, the levels are not printed on the passages. Instead, at the top of the page is a set of books with a specific pattern that will allow you to quickly match students and passages.

Pattern			
Reading Level	**easy** (below grade level)	**average** (at grade level)	**challenging** (above grade level)

Introduction (cont.)

Essential Comprehension Skills

Comprehension is the primary goal of any reading task. Students who comprehend expository text not only do better on tests, but they also have more opportunities in life. *Differentiated Nonfiction Reading* will help you to promote the foundation of comprehension skills necessary for a lifetime of learning. The questions following each passage always appear in the same order and cover six vital comprehension skills:

1. **Locating facts**—Questions based on exactly what the text states—*who, what, when, where, why,* and *how many*

2. **Understanding vocabulary in context**—Questions based on the ability to infer word meaning from the syntax and semantics of the surrounding text, as well as the ability to recognize known synonyms and antonyms for a newly encountered word

3. **Determining sequence**—Questions based on chronological order—what happened *first, last,* and *in between*

4. **Identifying conditions**—Questions that ask students to identify similarities and differences or notice cause-and-effect relationships

5. **Making inferences**—Questions that require students to evaluate, make decisions, and draw logical conclusions

6. **Analyzing and visualizing**—Questions that make students draw upon their schema and/or visualization skills to select the correct response (Visualization reinforces the important skill of picturing the text.)

How to Use This Book

You can choose to do whole-class or independent practice. For whole-group practice, you can:

1. Distribute the passages based on students' instructional reading levels.

2. Have students read the text silently and answer the questions either on the comprehension questions page or on one of the Answer Sheets on pages 94–95.

3. Collect all of the papers and score them.

4. Return the comprehension questions pages or Answer Sheets to the students, and discuss how they determined their answers.

5. Point out how students had to use their background knowledge to answer certain questions.

You may distribute the passages without revealing the different levels. There are several ways to approach this. If you do not want your students to be aware that the passages are differentiated, organize the passages in small piles by seating arrangement. Then, when you approach a group of desks, you have just the levels you need. An alternative is to make a pile of passages from diamonds to polka dots. Put a finger between the top two levels. Then, as you approach each student, pull the passage from the top (easy), middle (average), or bottom (challenging) layer. You will need to do this quickly and without much hesitation.

Introduction (cont.)

How to Use This Book (cont.)

You can also announce to your class that all students will read at their own instructional levels. Do not discuss the technicalities of how the reading levels were determined. Just state that every person is reading at his or her own level and then answering the same questions. By making this statement, you can make distributing the three different levels a straightforward process.

If you find that a student is doing well, try giving him or her the next-level-up passage the next time. If he or she displays frustration, be ready to slip the student the lower-level passage.

If you prefer to have the students work independently or in centers, follow this procedure:

1. Create a folder for each student.

2. If needed, make photocopies of the Answer Sheet on page 95 for each class member, and staple the Answer Sheet to the back of each student folder.

3. Each time you want to use a passage, place the appropriate reading level of the passage and the associated comprehension questions in each student's folder.

4. Have students retrieve their folders, read the passage, and answer the questions.

5. Go over the answers with the whole class, or check the folders individually at a convenient time.

6. As an option, you may want to provide a laminated copy of the Answer Key on page 96 in the center, so students can check their own papers.

Teaching Multiple-Choice Response

Whichever method you choose for using this book, it's a good idea to practice as a class how to read a passage and respond to the comprehension questions. In this way, you can demonstrate your own thought processes by "thinking aloud" to figure out an answer. Essentially, this means that you tell your students your thoughts as they come to you.

First, make copies of the practice comprehension questions on page 8, and distribute them to your class. Then, make and display an overhead transparency of the practice reading passage on page 7. Next, read the passage chorally. Studies have found that students of all ages enjoy choral reading, and it is especially helpful for English language learners. Choral reading lets students practice reading fluently in a safe venue because they can read in a whisper or even drop out if they feel the need.

Discuss Question 1: After you've read the passage aloud, ask a student to read the first question aloud. Tell the student NOT to answer the question. Instead, read all of the answer choices aloud. Emphasize that reading the choices first is always the best way to approach any multiple-choice question. Since this question is about *locating facts*, reread the first paragraph of the passage aloud as the class follows along. Have the students reread the question silently and make a selection based on the information found. Ask a student who gives the correct response (C) to explain his or her reasoning. Explain that the first question is always the easiest because the fact is stated right in the passage.

Teaching Multiple-Choice Response (cont.)

Discuss Question 2: The second question is about the *vocabulary* word shown in boldfaced print in the passage. Ask the student to read the question aloud. Teach your students to reread the sentence before, the sentence with, and the sentence after the vocabulary word in the passage. This will give them a context and help them to figure out what the word means. Then, have them substitute the word choices given for the vocabulary term in the passage. For each choice, they should reread the sentence with the substituted word and ask themselves, "Does this make sense?" This will help them to identify the best choice. One by one, substitute the words into the sentence, and read the sentence aloud. It will be obvious which one makes the most sense (A).

Discuss Question 3: The third question asks about *sequence*. Ask a student to read the question aloud. Write the choices on chart paper or the board. As a class, determine their order of occurrence, and write the numbers one through four next to them. Then, reread the question and make the correct choice (B).

Discuss Question 4: The fourth question is about *cause and effect* or *similarities and differences*. Ask a student to read the question aloud. Teach your students to look for the key words in the question ("pump water down") and search for those specific words in the passage. Explain that they may need to look for synonyms for the key words. For this question, ask your students to show where they found the correct response in the passage. Have students explain in their own words how they figured out the correct answer (D). This may be time-consuming at first, but it is an excellent way to help your students learn from each other.

Discuss Question 5: The fifth question asks students to make an *inference*. Ask the student to read the question aloud. Tell your students your thoughts as they occur to you, such as: "Well, the article didn't say that it is free to generate geothermal power, so that one's questionable. The article did say that geothermal energy comes from Earth, not from the sun, air, and water. So I'll get rid of that choice. We do have a lot of water, and in most places, that's what is forced down into Earth to make the steam. But you need to have a place where Earth is really hot near its surface, so it's not just a matter of having a water supply. I don't think that's the best choice here. Let's look back at the passage . . . it does state that there's an endless amount of heat rising from Earth, and we know that fossil fuels will soon be used up. Something that's endless cannot be used up, so I'm going to select D."

Discuss Question 6: The sixth question calls for *analysis* or *visualization*. With such questions, some of the answers may be stated in the passage, but others may have different wording. Sometimes one or more of the answers must be visualized to ascertain the correct response.

After having a student read the question aloud, you can say, "This one is tricky. It's asking me to choose the one that *isn't* instead of the one that *is*. First, let's look at all the choices. Then, we can ask ourselves which ones are problems with geothermal power. Only one of these is not an issue." Then, read the answer choices aloud and eliminate them one by one. Point out that the passage states that geothermal energy does not pollute groundwater, which is how you identify the correct answer (C).

Frequent Practice Is Ideal

The passages and comprehension questions in *Differentiated Nonfiction Reading* are time-efficient, allowing your students to practice these skills often. The more your students practice reading and responding to content-area comprehension questions, the more confident and competent they will become. Set aside time to allow your class to do every passage. If you do so, you'll be pleased with your students' improved comprehension of any nonfiction text, both within your classroom and beyond its walls.

Geothermal Power

Our Earth has a layer of hot rock below its crust in an area called the mantle. Where groundwater touches these hot rocks, it changes into steam. This steam enables people to make electricity without causing pollution. It's called geothermal power. *Geo* means Earth, and *thermal* means heat.

Italians built the first geothermal power station in 1904. They found a place where steam rose from the ground. They trapped the steam and sent it through pipes to turbines. Turbines are big and round and can spin very quickly. The steam made the turbines turn, which **generated** electrical power.

In most places, steam does not come up on its own. Instead, power stations pump water down to the mantle. Some of this water returns as steam to make turbines rotate and create electricity.

Geothermal energy is good for Earth and its wildlife. It does not damage the air, water, or soil. However, the steam can bring up minerals that harm the turbines. Also, workers must be careful around the steam, or they could get burned.

Someday all of the fossil fuels will be used up. Geothermal power can never get used up. That's why people hope to find more places and better ways to use geothermal power.

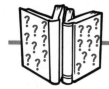

Geothermal Power

Directions: Darken the best answer choice.

1. "Geothermal" means _____ from Earth.
   - Ⓐ steam
   - Ⓑ energy
   - Ⓒ heat
   - Ⓓ water

2. The word **generated** means
   - Ⓐ made.
   - Ⓑ used.
   - Ⓒ opened.
   - Ⓓ wasted.

3. Of the following choices, which occurs last?
   - Ⓐ Steam moves turbines.
   - Ⓑ Electricity goes to homes.
   - Ⓒ Steam is trapped in pipes.
   - Ⓓ Electrical power is made.

4. Why would people pump water down to a layer of hot rock?
   - Ⓐ to cool Earth's mantle
   - Ⓑ to prevent steam from escaping
   - Ⓒ to bring minerals to Earth's surface
   - Ⓓ to create steam

5. Why can't geothermal power get used up as fossil fuels can?
   - Ⓐ It costs nothing to generate geothermal power.
   - Ⓑ Scientists know how to make geothermal energy from the sun, air, and water.
   - Ⓒ We have a huge supply of water, which is what gives us geothermal power.
   - Ⓓ There's an endless supply of heat coming from within Earth.

6. Which is *not* a problem related to geothermal power?
   - Ⓐ Minerals can build up on the turbines.
   - Ⓑ There are just a few places to tap the power.
   - Ⓒ It causes salt to build up and damage the groundwater.
   - Ⓓ The steam is dangerous if it comes in contact with workers.

Standards Correlation

Each passage and comprehension question in *Differentiated Nonfiction Reading* meets at least one of the following standards and benchmarks, which are used with permission from McREL. Copyright 2010 McREL. Mid-continent Research for Education and Learning, 4601 DTC Boulevard, Suite 500, Denver, CO 80237. Telephone: 303-337-0990. Web site: *www.mcrel.org/standards-benchmarks*

Standards and Benchmarks	Passage Title	Pages
SCIENCE		
Standard 5. Understands the structure and function of cells and organisms **Benchmark 1.** Knows that plants and animals progress through life cycles of birth, growth and development, reproduction, and death; the details of these life cycles are different for different organisms **Benchmark 2.** Knows that living organisms have distinct structures and body systems that serve specific functions in growth, survival, and reproduction	Beavers: Master Builders Fascinating Flies	14–17 18–21
Standard 6. Understands relationships among organisms and their physical environment **Benchmark 2.** Knows that living things are found almost everywhere in the world and that distinct environments support the life of different types of plants and animals **Benchmark 4.** Knows that changes in the environment can have different effects on different organisms **Benchmark 5.** Knows that all organisms (including humans) cause changes in their environments and these changes can be beneficial or detrimental	Beavers: Master Builders Dr. Ruth Patrick, Water Pioneer	14–17 26–29
Standard 7. Understands biological evolution and the diversity of life **Benchmark 2.** Knows different ways in which living things can be grouped (e.g., plants/animals, bones/no bones, insects/spiders, live on land/live in water) and the purposes of different groupings	Fascinating Flies	18–21
Standard 9. Understands the sources and properties of energy **Benchmark 1.** Knows that heat is often produced as a byproduct when one form of energy is converted to another form **Benchmark 2.** Knows that heat can move from one object to another by conduction and that some materials conduct heat better than others	Heat	22–25
Standard 12. Understands the nature of scientific inquiry **Benchmark 1.** Knows that learning can come from careful observations and simple experiments **Benchmark 2.** Knows that tools (e.g., thermometers, magnifiers, rulers, balances) can be used to gather information and extend the senses	Dr. Ruth Patrick, Water Pioneer	26–29

Standards Correlation (cont.)

Standards and Benchmarks	Passage Title	Pages
SCIENCE (cont.)		
Standard 13. Understands the scientific enterprise **Benchmark 1.** Knows that people of all ages, backgrounds, and groups have made contributions to science and technology throughout history	Dr. Ruth Patrick, Water Pioneer	26–29
Benchmark 3. Knows that scientists and engineers often work in teams to accomplish a task	Bill Gates, Inventor and Humanitarian	30–33
GEOGRAPHY		
Standard 7. Knows the physical processes that shape patterns on Earth's surface **Benchmark 1.** Knows the physical components of Earth's atmosphere (e.g., weather and climate), lithosphere (e.g., landforms such as mountains, hills, plateaus, plains), hydrosphere (e.g., oceans, lakes, rivers), and biosphere (e.g., vegetation and biomes) **Benchmark 2.** Understands how physical processes help to shape features and patterns on Earth's surface (e.g., the effects of climate and weather on vegetation, erosion and deposition on landforms, mudslides on hills)	Sinkholes	34–37
Standard 9. Understands the nature, distribution, and migration of human populations on Earth's surface **Benchmark 3.** Understands voluntary and involuntary migration **Benchmark 4.** Knows the causes and effects of human migration (e.g., European colonists and African slaves to America, movement of people from drought areas in Africa, movement of people from East Asia to North America, effects of physical geography on national and international migration, cultural factors)	The Legacy of Turkey Red Wheat	38–41
Standard 14. Understands how human actions modify the physical environment **Benchmark 1.** Knows the ways people alter the physical environment (e.g., by creating irrigation projects; clearing the land to make room for houses and shopping centers; planting crops; building roads) **Benchmark 2.** Knows the ways in which the physical environment is stressed by human activities (e.g., changes in climate, air pollution, water pollution, expanding human settlement) **Benchmark 3.** Knows how human activities have increased the ability of the physical environment to support human life in the local community, state, United States, and other countries	People Affect Water	42–45

Standards Correlation (cont.)

Standards and Benchmarks	Passage Title	Pages
GEOGRAPHY (cont.)		
Standard 15. Understands how physical systems affect human systems **Benchmark 4.** Knows natural hazards that occur in the physical environment (e.g., floods, windstorms, tornadoes, earthquakes)	A Natural Disaster: Hurricane Katrina	46–49
Standard 16. Understands the changes that occur in the meaning, use, distribution, and importance of resources **Benchmark 1.** Knows the characteristics, location, and use of renewable resources (e.g., timber), flow resources (e.g., running water or wind), and nonrenewable resources (e.g., fossil fuels, minerals)	Is That the Wind? No, It's Energy!	50–53
HISTORY		
Standard 2. Understands the history of a local community and how communities in North America varied long ago **Benchmark 4.** Understands the challenges and difficulties encountered by people in pioneer farming communities (e.g., the Old Northwest, the prairies, the Southwest, eastern Canada, the Far West)	The Legacy of Turkey Red Wheat	38–41
Standard 3. Understands the people, events, problems, and ideas that were significant in creating the history of their state **Benchmark 3.** Understands the interactions that occurred between the Native Americans or Hawaiians and the first European, African, and Asian-Pacific explorers and settlers in the state or region	Different Viewpoints in History	58–61
Standard 4. Understands how democratic values came to be, and how they have been exemplified by people, events, and symbols **Benchmark 3.** Understands how people over the last 200 years have continued to struggle to bring to all groups in American society the liberties and equality promised in the basic principles of American democracy	Different Viewpoints in History	58–61
Benchmark 4. Understands the accomplishments of ordinary people in historical situations and how each struggled for individual rights or for the common good	Jane Addams, Social Reformer	54–57
Benchmark 6. Understands historical figures who believed in the fundamental democratic values (e.g., justice, truth, equality, the rights of the individual, responsibility for the common good, voting rights) and the significance of these people both in their historical context and today	Colin Powell, Former U.S. Secretary of State	62–65

Standards Correlation (cont.)

Standards and Benchmarks	Passage Title	Pages
HISTORY (cont.)		
Standard 4. (cont.) **Benchmark 7.** Understands how historical figures in the U.S. and in other parts of the world have advanced the rights of individuals and promoted the common good, and the character traits that made them successful	Colin Powell, Former U.S. Secretary of State	62–65
Benchmark 14. Understands how people have helped make the community a better place to live (e.g., working to preserve the environment, helping the homeless, restoring houses in low-income areas)	Bill Gates, Inventor and Humanitarian Jane Addams, Social Reformer	30–33 54–57
Standard 8. Understands major discoveries in science and technology, some of their social and economic effects, and the major scientists and inventors responsible for them **Benchmark 12.** Understands the significance of the printing press, the computer, and electronic developments in communication and their impact on the spread of ideas **Benchmark 13.** Knows about people who have made significant contributions in the field of communications (e.g., the inventors of the telegraph, telephone, the Braille alphabet, radio, television, the computer, satellite communication)	Satellites Bill Gates, Inventor and Humanitarian Helping the Blind and Deaf Communicate	70–73 30–33 66–69
LANGUAGE ARTS*		
Standard 7. Uses reading skills and strategies to understand and interpret a variety of informational texts **Benchmark 1.** Uses reading skills and strategies to understand a variety of informational texts (e.g., textbooks, biographical sketches, letters, diaries, directions, procedures, magazines) **Benchmark 2.** Knows the defining characteristics of a variety of informational texts (e.g., textbooks, biographical sketches, letters, diaries, directions, procedures, magazines) **Benchmark 3.** Uses text organizers (e.g., headings, topic and summary sentences, graphic features, typeface, chapter titles) to determine the main ideas and to locate information in a text **Benchmark 6.** Uses prior knowledge and experience to understand and respond to new information **Benchmark 7.** Understands structural patterns or organization in informational texts (chronological, logical, or sequential order; compare-and-contrast; cause-and-effect; proposition and support)	First Flight (Vacation Blog) The Wandering Rocks of Death Valley (Tourist Guide) When Booth Saved Lincoln's Life (Magazine Feature) The World's Most Mysterious Places (Back of Book) Getting to Know Your Chinchilla (Web Site)	74–77 78–81 82–85 86–89 90–93

*Each passage in this book meets the language arts standard of some or all of these benchmarks. The language arts passages are listed here because they were designed to specifically address these benchmarks.

Reading Levels Chart

Content Area and Title	Easy ◆	Average ★	Challenging ●
SCIENCE			
Beavers: Master Builders	3.3	4.6	5.7
Fascinating Flies	3.6	4.6	5.5
Heat	3.0	4.3	5.3
Dr. Ruth Patrick, Water Pioneer	3.0	4.2	5.1
Bill Gates, Inventor and Humanitarian	3.7	4.7	5.8
GEOGRAPHY			
Sinkholes	3.0	4.2	5.5
The Legacy of Turkey Red Wheat	3.6	4.6	5.7
People Affect Water	3.7	4.6	5.7
A Natural Disaster: Hurricane Katrina	3.6	4.7	5.8
Is That the Wind? No, It's Energy!	3.3	4.1	5.6
HISTORY			
Jane Addams, Social Reformer	3.4	4.6	5.7
Different Viewpoints in History	3.3	4.3	5.7
Colin Powell, Former U.S. Secretary of State	3.7	4.7	5.7
Helping the Blind and Deaf Communicate	3.3	4.2	5.4
Satellites	3.5	4.6	5.5
LANGUAGE ARTS			
First Flight (Vacation Blog)	3.0	4.5	5.7
The Wandering Rocks of Death Valley (Tourist Guide)	3.5	4.6	5.5
When Booth Saved Lincoln's Life (Magazine Feature)	3.4	4.6	5.8
The World's Most Mysterious Places (Back of Book)	3.3	4.5	5.7
Getting to Know Your Chinchilla (Web Site)	3.1	4.1	5.4

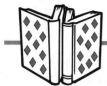

Beavers: Master Builders

Beavers are the only animals (besides us) who act to change their environment in a major way. Beavers build dams in streams to create ponds. They want a small body of water with a stable, year-round water level. The water must be at least two-and-a-half feet deep. That's because beavers eat plants that grow underwater. They also eat and use young trees. When a beaver blocks a stream, it not only makes a pond, but it helps form wetlands. Wetlands support many plants and animals. Almost half of all the endangered species in North America live in wetlands. These areas filter dirt from water. They absorb extra water during floods, too.

Beavers build dams to create standing water, but that's not all they build. They make big lodges for homes. A lodge starts out as a bank den. It is a hole dug into the bank of a river or a stream. The beavers tunnel up to above the waterline. Then, they top the bank den with mud, sticks, and rocks. They live in the den while they build the dam. The dam forms a body of water around the den. Next, they enlarge the den. It becomes a lodge. To make a dam or a lodge, a beaver needs a lot of wood. It chops down young trees with its sharp, orange teeth. (To keep its balance while doing this, the beaver uses its big, flat tail like a fifth leg.)

As animal homes go, beaver lodges are mansions. Inside the lodge is a warm, dry chamber. Here, the beavers sleep and raise their young. Lodges are used for many years unless wrecked by flood, fire, or humans. To **thwart** predators, such as lynx, beaver homes have only underwater openings. There is at least one exit into deep water. The beavers do not want to get trapped inside when ice forms on the pond.

The beaver is North America's biggest rodent. Even so, it's not common to see one. They come out mostly at night. A beaver can live twelve years. It can grow up to four feet long. Adults weigh between forty and seventy pounds. They live in family groups of parents and offspring. Adults mate for life. Each year, they have two to four kits. When a kit reaches the age of two or three, it finds a mate. Together, they build their own dam and lodge. Sometimes they make their lodge in another part of the parents' pond.

Beavers are great swimmers. They use their strong tails to steer underwater. A beaver can hold its breath. It can stay underwater for fifteen minutes. Valves in the nose keep water from getting into the lungs. They have valves in their ears, too. An adult's tail is about ten inches long and six inches wide. If a beaver sees a predator, it slaps its tail on the water. The sound warns other beavers. They are in danger while on land. They try to stay within sixty-five feet of the shore at all times.

Do all the mud-and-stick lodges that you see in ponds belong to beavers? No. They may be muskrat lodges. Muskrats are common. They are the most abundant fur-bearing animals in the United States. But they do not create ponds. They just build lodges in ponds that are already there.

Beavers: Master Builders

Beavers are the only animals (besides humans) who deliberately make a major change to the environment. Beavers build dams to maintain a stable, year-round water level that's at least two-and-a-half feet deep. That's because beavers eat plants that grow underwater. They also eat young trees, or saplings. When a beaver blocks a stream, it not only makes a pond, but it also creates wetlands that support a lot of plants and animals. In fact, nearly half of all the endangered species in North America live in wetlands. These areas filter toxins from water and absorb excess water during floods as well.

Beavers build dams to create standing water, but that's not all they build. They make elaborate lodges for homes. A lodge starts out as a bank den. It is a hole dug into the bank of running water, such as a river or a stream. The beavers tunnel up to above the waterline. They top the bank den with mud, sticks, and rocks. Then, they build the dam to create a body of water around the den. Next, they build the den into a lodge. To make a dam or a lodge, a beaver needs a lot of wood. It must chop down aspen and birch saplings with its sharp, orange teeth. (To keep its balance while doing this, the beaver uses its large, flat tail like a fifth leg.)

As animal homes go, beaver lodges are mansions. Inside each one is a warm, dry chamber. This is where the beavers sleep and raise their young. Lodges are used for many years unless destroyed by flood, fire, or humans. To **thwart** predators, such as lynx, there are only underwater openings into a beaver home. There is at least one exit into deep water. This is to be sure that the beavers never get trapped inside by ice in the winter.

The beaver is North America's largest rodent, but it's not common to see one because they are nocturnal. A beaver can live twelve years and grow up to four feet long. Adults weigh between forty and seventy pounds. They live in family groups made up of the parents and offspring. Adults mate for life. Each year, between two and four kits are born. When a kit reaches two or three years old, it finds a mate. Together, they build their own dam and lodge. Sometimes they make their lodge in another part of the parents' pond.

Beavers are expert swimmers. They use their strong tails to steer underwater. A beaver can hold its breath and stay underwater for fifteen minutes. Valves in the nose keep water from flowing into the lungs. Valves in the ears keep that part dry as well. An adult's tail is about ten inches long and six inches wide. If a beaver sees a predator, it slaps its tail on the water as a warning to other beavers. They are in danger while on land and try to stay within sixty-five feet of the shore.

Do all the mud-and-stick lodges that you see in ponds belong to beavers? No. They may be muskrat lodges. Muskrats are common. They are the most abundant fur-bearing animals in the United States. However, they never create ponds. They just build lodges in ponds that are already there.

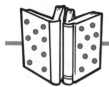

Beavers: Master Builders

Beavers are the only animals (besides humans) that deliberately and drastically change their environment. Beavers build dams to maintain a stable, year-round water level that's at least two-and-a-half feet deep. That's because beavers eat plants that grow underwater. They also eat young trees, or saplings. When a beaver blocks a stream, it not only makes a pond, but it also creates wetlands. This supports a wide variety of plants and animals. Nearly half of all the endangered species in North America live in wetlands. These areas filter toxins from water and absorb excess water during floods, too.

Beavers build dams to create standing water, but that's not all they build. They make elaborate lodges for homes. A lodge starts out as a bank den. It is a hole dug into the bank of running water, such as a river or a stream. The beavers tunnel up to above the waterline and top the bank den with mud, sticks, and rocks. Then, they build the dam to create a body of water to surround the den. Next, they build the den into a lodge. To construct a dam or a lodge, a beaver needs a lot of wood. It chops down aspen and birch saplings using its sharp, orange teeth. (To keep its balance while felling timber, the beaver uses its large, flat tail like an extra leg.)

As animal homes go, beaver lodges are mansions: inside each one is a warm, dry chamber where the beavers sleep and raise their young. Lodges are used for many years unless destroyed by flood, fire, or humans. To **thwart** predators, such as lynx, beaver homes only have underwater openings, with at least one exit into deep water. This is to be sure that the beavers never get trapped inside by ice in the winter.

The beaver is North America's largest rodent, but it's relatively uncommon to see one because they are nocturnal. A beaver can live twelve years and grow up to four feet long. Adults weigh between forty and seventy pounds. They live in family groups consisting of the parents and offspring. Adults mate for life. Each year between two and four kits are born. When a kit reaches two or three years old, it finds a mate, and together they build their own dam and lodge. Occasionally, they make their lodge in another part of the parents' pond.

Beavers are expert swimmers, using their powerful tails to steer underwater. A beaver can hold its breath and stay underwater for fifteen minutes. Valves in the nose and ears keep water from flowing into the body. An adult's tail is about ten inches long and six inches wide. If a beaver sees a predator, it slaps its tail on the water. This serves as a warning to other beavers. They are only in danger while on land and try to stay within sixty-five feet of the shore.

Do all mud-and-stick lodges that you see in ponds belong to beavers? No. They may be muskrat lodges. Muskrats are the most abundant fur-bearing animals in the United States. However, they never create ponds; they just build lodges in ponds that are already there.

Beavers: Master Builders

Directions: Darken the best answer choice.

1. Which statement is true?
   Ⓐ Beavers eat small fish.
   Ⓑ Beavers are most active at night.
   Ⓒ Beavers cannot walk on land.
   Ⓓ Beavers hibernate during the winter.

2. The word **thwart** means
   Ⓐ prevent.
   Ⓑ assist.
   Ⓒ detect.
   Ⓓ imitate.

3. Which event happens third?
   Ⓐ The beavers build a bank den.
   Ⓑ Two beavers choose each other as mates.
   Ⓒ The beavers build a dam to create a pond.
   Ⓓ The beavers change the bank den into a lodge.

4. How do beavers differ from muskrats?
   Ⓐ Beavers have more fur than muskrats.
   Ⓑ Muskrats live longer than beavers do.
   Ⓒ Adult beavers are smaller than adult muskrats.
   Ⓓ Beavers create ponds and muskrats do not.

5. Which is most apt to wreck a beaver lodge?
   Ⓐ a lynx digging its way through
   Ⓑ a big flood
   Ⓒ a park created to protect wetlands
   Ⓓ a snapping turtle destroying the lodge from within

6. It is just after dusk, and you are near the shore of a pond. You see a beaver on the far bank. What is it probably doing?
   Ⓐ fighting a muskrat
   Ⓑ slapping its tail on the land
   Ⓒ teaching its young to swim
   Ⓓ chewing on young birch trees

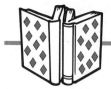

Fascinating Flies

Insects are some of the most successful animals on Earth. They can survive in tough conditions. They reproduce in huge quantities. It has been said that without insects, few of us would be alive. Why? They are near the start of many food chains. They provide food for other animals. And yet, we mostly think of insects as pests.

All mammals, amphibians, reptiles, and fish have internal skeletons. They are made of bones. Each insect has an exoskeleton. It is a structure on the outside of the body. It has no bones, yet it gives the body its form. Some insects have wings. Others don't. All insects have antennae and six legs. They also have three body parts: a head, a thorax, and an abdomen. The legs and wings attach to the thorax. The digestive and reproductive systems are within the abdomen.

Flies are some of the most common insects. The housefly has been around for sixty-five million years! That means it survived whatever conditions killed the dinosaurs. The housefly goes through four stages of development: egg, larva, pupa, and adult. Going from egg to adult takes just ten days. Females can lay 2,500 eggs in one month. The larvae eat solids like trash, rotting plants, and animal waste. An adult fly can only suck up liquids. When you see a fly land on something and move its legs about, it is **analyzing** the surface to see if there is any fluid. After reaching the adult stage, flies can live for sixty days. They beat their wings up to 200 times per second. This lets them fly up to forty-five miles per hour. They have two main eyes. There are 4,000 smaller eyes within each eye.

Housefly

Have you ever been bitten by a huge fly? The spot can itch for days. Houseflies do not bite. You were probably bitten by a female horsefly. Horseflies look like huge houseflies. Their antennae look like horns. They live near areas with water and livestock. Adult females drink the blood of large mammals (like cows, horses, and humans). They need blood in order to lay eggs. Adult males drink nectar from flowers or suck juices from fruit. The horsefly goes through the same stages of development as the housefly. The female lays her eggs on plants in a marsh or a swamp. After an egg hatches, the larva spends up to two years growing in moist soil near the water. As a larva, it eats other bugs, worms, and even tiny fish! It becomes a pupa during the winter. Once a horsefly becomes an adult, it has one week to live. The females rush to mate, drink blood, and lay eggs.

Horsefly

The crane fly doesn't look like a fly. It looks like a huge mosquito. It goes through the same stages of growth as other flies. It lays eggs on water plants or in damp soil. After seventy-two hours, the eggs hatch as larvae. It takes one month for the larvae to change into pupae and then into adults. As a larva, it eats roots and rotting leaves. Once the crane fly becomes an adult, it never eats again! That's because it only lives for three days. It must hurry to mate and lay eggs before it dies.

Crane fly

Fascinating Flies

Insects are some of the most successful animals on Earth. They survive in extreme conditions and reproduce in huge quantities. It can be argued that without insects, few of us would survive. Why? They are near the start of many food chains, providing food for other animals. And yet, we usually think of insects only as pests.

All mammals, amphibians, reptiles, and fish have internal skeletons made of bones. Insects do not. Instead, each one has an exoskeleton, which is a structure on the outside of the body. An exoskeleton has no bones, yet it gives the body its form. Some insects have wings. All insects have antennae and six legs. They also have three body parts: a head, a thorax, and an abdomen. The legs and wings attach to the thorax, while the digestive and reproductive systems are within the abdomen.

Flies are some of the most common insects. The housefly has been around for sixty-five million years, which means it survived whatever conditions killed the dinosaurs. The housefly goes through four stages of development: egg, larva, pupa, and adult. Changing from egg to adult takes just ten days. Females can lay 2,500 eggs in one month. The larvae eat solids such as trash, rotting plants, and animal waste. However, an adult fly can only suck up liquids. When you see a fly land on something and move its legs about, it is **analyzing** the surface to see if there is any fluid. After reaching the adult stage, flies can live for sixty days. Houseflies can beat their wings 200 times per second, letting them fly up to forty-five miles per hour. They have two main eyes, with 4,000 smaller eyes within each eye.

Housefly

Have you ever been bitten by a huge fly? The spot can itch for days. But houseflies do not bite. You were probably bitten by a female horsefly. Horseflies look like gigantic houseflies with horn-like

Horsefly

antennae. They live near areas with water and livestock. Adult females must drink the blood of large mammals (like horses, cows, and humans). They need blood in order to lay eggs. Adult males drink nectar from flowers or suck juices from fruit. The horsefly goes through the same stages of development as the housefly. The female lays her eggs on plants in a marsh or a swamp. After an egg hatches, the larva spends up to two years growing in moist soil near the water. As a larva, it eats other bugs, worms, and even tiny fish! It becomes a pupa during the winter. Once a horsefly becomes an adult, it has one week to live. The females rush to mate, drink blood, and lay eggs.

The crane fly doesn't look like a fly; it looks like a gigantic mosquito. It goes through the same stages of development as other flies. It lays eggs on water plants or in moist soil. After seventy-two hours, the eggs hatch as larvae. It takes one month for the larvae to change into pupae and then into adults. As a larva, it eats roots and rotting leaves. Once the crane fly reaches adulthood, it never eats again! That's because it only lives for three days. It must hurry to mate and lay eggs before it dies.

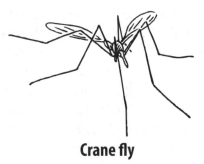

Crane fly

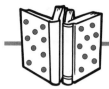

Fascinating Flies

Insects are some of Earth's most successful animals. They survive in extreme conditions and reproduce in huge quantities. Without insects, few of us would survive since they are near the start of many food chains and provide food for other animals. And yet, we usually think of insects only as pests.

All mammals, amphibians, reptiles, and fish have internal skeletons made of bones, but insects do not. Instead, each one has an exoskeleton, which is a structure on the outside of the body. An exoskeleton has no bones, yet it gives the body its form. Some insects have wings. All insects have antennae and six legs as well as three body parts: a head, a thorax, and an abdomen. The legs and wings attach to the thorax, while the digestive and reproductive systems are housed within the abdomen.

Flies are some of the most common insects. The housefly has been around for sixty-five million years, which means it survived whatever conditions killed the dinosaurs. The housefly goes through four stages of development: egg, larva, pupa, and adult. Changing from egg to adult takes just ten days. Females can lay 2,500 eggs per month. The eggs turn into larvae, which eat solids such as trash, rotting plants, and animal waste. An adult fly can only suck up liquids, so when you see a fly land on something and move its legs, it is **analyzing** the surface to see if there is any fluid. After reaching the adult stage, houseflies can live for sixty days. They can beat their wings 200 times per second, which allows them to fly up to forty-five miles per hour. They have two main eyes, with 4,000 smaller eyes within each eye.

Housefly

Have you ever been bitten by a huge fly? The spot can itch for days. But a housefly wasn't the culprit because they do not bite. You were probably bitten by a female horsefly. Horseflies look like gigantic houseflies with horn-like antennae. They live near water and livestock. Adult females must drink the blood of large mammals (like horses, cows, and humans) in order to lay eggs. Adult males drink nectar from flowers or suck juices from fruit. The horsefly goes through the same stages of development as the housefly. The female lays her eggs on plants in a marsh or a swamp. After an egg hatches, the larva spends up to two years growing in moist soil near the water eating bugs, worms, and even tiny fish! It becomes a pupa during the winter. Once a horsefly becomes an adult, it has just one week to live. The females rush to mate, drink blood, and lay eggs.

Horsefly

The crane fly doesn't look one bit like a fly; it looks like a gigantic mosquito. It goes through the same stages of development as other flies. It lays its eggs on water plants or in moist soil, and after seventy-two hours, the eggs hatch as larvae. It takes one month for the larvae to change into pupae and then adults. As a larva, it eats roots and rotting leaves. Once the crane fly reaches adulthood, it never eats again because it only lives for three days. It must hurry to mate and lay eggs before it dies.

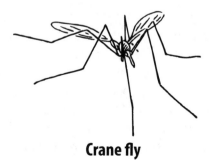

Crane fly

Fascinating Flies

Directions: Darken the best answer choice.

1. Is there a stage during which a housefly can eat solids?
   Ⓐ Yes, in the larva stage a housefly eats solids.
   Ⓑ Yes, in the adult stage a housefly eats solids.
   Ⓒ Yes, in the pupa stage a housefly eats solids.
   Ⓓ No, a housefly can never eat solids.

2. The word **analyzing** means
   Ⓐ changing.
   Ⓑ examining.
   Ⓒ completing.
   Ⓓ stirring.

3. A female horsefly has just changed from a pupa to an adult. What is the second thing she does?
   Ⓐ She drinks flowers' nectar.
   Ⓑ She mates with a male horsefly.
   Ⓒ She drinks mammals' blood.
   Ⓓ She lays eggs in moist soil.

4. Which fly has the longest adult life span?
   Ⓐ horsefly
   Ⓑ crane fly
   Ⓒ housefly
   Ⓓ They all have the same adult life span.

5. Which of these is *not* a fly body part?
   Ⓐ a skeleton
   Ⓑ antennae
   Ⓒ an abdomen
   Ⓓ a thorax

6. If you see a male horsefly drinking, he is probably sucking
   Ⓐ the fluids in animal waste.
   Ⓑ the juice of a cherry.
   Ⓒ a horse's blood.
   Ⓓ fluids from dead animals.

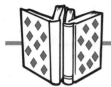

Heat

If you lift the hood of a car when the motor is running, you must not touch the engine, even though it is now shut off. Why? It might burn your hand! The engine is hot because it has been running. When energy is **converted** from one form to another, heat is always created. It may be a lot or a little heat. Changing energy from one form to another results in some loss, too. The amount of energy stays the same. But not all of the energy changes into the form we want. Thus, when gas burns to make a car go, some of the energy is lost. It goes out of the exhaust pipe. The same is true of a furnace. It heats a home. The more efficient a device is, the more the energy changes into what we want. For example, a 95-percent-efficient furnace means that just 5 percent of the gas or oil it burns will be lost. This 5 percent goes out the flue.* The rest will turn into heat for the home.

The most efficient cars get the most miles from a gallon of gas. It means changing the gas into motion with the smallest possible heat loss. We'd like it if every drop of gas went toward moving the wheels. We may never be able to design such vehicles. But engineers are working on this goal.

Heat moves from one thing to another by conduction. Some objects conduct heat quickly and easily. Others do not. Suppose you need to take a hot pan from the oven. You use a potholder. It protects your hand. The heat does not move from the pan through the cloth very quickly. But if you used a wet potholder, your hand would be burned. Why? Damp cloth conducts heat almost instantly. Some materials do not conduct heat at all. Instead, the heat wrecks them. When exposed to heat, they melt or burn. Soft plastic will melt. Paper will burn.

Metal conducts heat easily. Metal also expands when heated. This can cause a problem for railroads. It is called a sun kink. In July 2002, an Amtrak train derailed near the nation's capital. It was due to a sun kink. It was a 100-degree day. The metal of the track absorbed the sun's heat. This made the metal's atoms move. The hotter it got, the faster they moved. They hit nearby atoms and pushed them away. This made the track bend several inches. The train left the tracks. After this accident, trains in the D.C. area were not allowed to run on such hot days. In other places with sun kinks, trains must slow to ten miles per hour on hot days. Scientists are trying to find a fix. They hope to design a fiberoptic cable. It will be affixed to the rails. It will ring an alarm as soon as a sun kink begins.

Have you ever seen swamp lights at night? They are strange, glowing lights near the ground in marshy, damp areas. They look spooky. Many people call them will-o'-the-wisps. The glow is from a very low form of heat. It comes from burning methane. Methane is an invisible gas. It rises from rotting plant matter. In damp places, dead plants and leaves rot quickly. Heat in the air or a lightning strike makes the methane burn. But it is a cool fire. It doesn't cause enough heat to start a blaze. The damp environment helps to prevent the fire from spreading, too.

*exhaust vent

Heat

Why is it that when a car's motor has been running, you must not touch the engine, even once it is shut off? It might burn your hand! The engine is hot because it has been running. When energy is **converted** from one form to another, heat is always created. It may not always be a lot of heat, but heat is generated. Changing energy from one form to another usually results in some loss as well. The amount of energy stays the same. Yet not all of the energy changes into the form we desire. Thus, when gas burns to make a car run, some of the energy is lost through the exhaust pipe. The same is true of a furnace used to heat a house. The more efficient a device is, the more the energy changes into what we want. For example, a 95-percent-efficient furnace means that 5 percent of the gas or oil it burns will go out the flue.* The rest will be used as heat for the home.

The most efficient cars are the ones that get the most miles from a gallon of gas. Again, it's a matter of changing the gas into motion with the smallest possible heat loss. We'd like it if every drop of gas went toward moving the wheels. We may never be able to design such efficient vehicles. But engineers are working on this goal.

Heat moves from one object to another by conduction. Some objects conduct heat quickly and easily; others do not. Suppose you need to take a hot pan out of the oven. You use a potholder to protect your hand. The heat does not travel from the pan through the cloth very quickly. However, if you used a wet potholder, your hand would be burned. Why? Damp cloth conducts heat almost instantly. Some materials do not conduct heat at all. Instead, the heat destroys them. When exposed to heat, they melt or burn. Soft plastic melts; paper burns.

Metal conducts heat easily. Metal also expands when heated. This can cause a major problem for railroads called a sun kink. In July 2002, an Amtrak train derailed near the nation's capital due to a sun kink. It was a 100-degree day. The metal of the track absorbed the sun's heat. This made the metal's atoms move faster and faster. They hit nearby atoms and pushed them away. This made the track actually bend several inches and caused the train to leave the tracks. After this accident, trains in the D.C. area were not allowed to run on such hot days. In other places with sun kinks, trains are slowed to ten miles per hour on hot days. Scientists are trying to design a fiberoptic cable that can be affixed to the rails and ring an alarm as soon as a sun kink begins.

Have you ever seen swamp lights at night? They are strange, glowing lights usually close to the ground in marshy, damp areas. They look spooky, and many people call them will-o'-the-wisps. A very low form of heat causes the glow. It comes from burning methane. Methane is an invisible gas. It comes from rotting plant matter. In damp places, dead plants and leaves decay quickly. Heat in the air or a lightning strike can cause the methane to burn. But it is a cool fire; it doesn't cause enough heat to start a blaze. The damp environment helps to keep the fire from spreading, too.

*exhaust vent

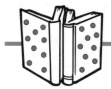

Heat

Why is it that when a car's motor has been running, you must not touch the engine, even once it is turned off? It might burn your hand! The engine is hot because it has been running. When energy is **converted** from one form to another, heat is always created. It may not always be a lot of heat, but heat is generated. Changing energy from one form to another usually results in some loss as well. Although the amount of energy stays the same, not all of the energy changes into the form we desire. Thus, when gas burns to make a car run, some of the energy gets lost through the exhaust pipe, and the same is true of a furnace used to heat a house. The more efficient a device is, the more the energy changes into what we want. For example, a 95-percent-efficient furnace means that just 5 percent of the gas or oil it burns will go out the flue.* The rest will be used as heat for the home.

The most efficient cars are the ones that get the most miles from a gallon of gas; it's a matter of changing the gas into motion with the smallest possible heat loss. We'd like it if every drop of gas went toward moving the wheels. We may never be able to design such efficient vehicles, but engineers are working on this goal.

Heat moves from one object to another by conduction. Some objects conduct heat quickly and easily; others do not. Suppose you need to take a hot pan out of the oven. You use a potholder to protect your hand because the heat does not travel from the pan through the cloth very quickly. However, if you used a wet potholder, your hand would be burned. Damp cloth conducts heat almost instantly. Some materials do not conduct heat at all; instead, the heat destroys them. When exposed to heat, they melt or burn. Soft plastic melts; paper burns.

Metal not only conducts heat easily, it expands when heated. This can cause a major problem for railroads called a sun kink. In July 2002, an Amtrak train derailed near the nation's capital due to a sun kink on a 100-degree day. The metal of the track absorbed the sun's heat, which made the metal's atoms move faster and faster. They hit nearby atoms and pushed them away. This made the track actually bend several inches and caused the train to leave the tracks. After this accident, trains in the D.C. area were not allowed to run on such hot days. In other places with sun kinks, trains are slowed to ten miles per hour on hot days. Scientists are trying to design a fiberoptic cable that can be affixed to the rails and ring an alarm as soon as a sun kink begins.

Have you ever seen swamp lights at night? They are strange, glowing lights usually close to the ground in marshy, damp areas. They look spooky, and many people call them will-o'-the-wisps. The glow comes from a very low form of heat that comes from burning methane. Methane is an invisible gas that rises from rotting plant matter. In damp places, dead plants and leaves decay quickly. Heat in the air or a lightning strike can cause the methane to burn. But it is a cool fire; it doesn't generate enough heat to start a blaze. The damp environment also helps to prevent the fire from spreading.

*exhaust vent

Heat

Directions: Darken the best answer choice.

1. Swamp lights are the result of
   Ⓐ heat conduction.
   Ⓑ sun kinks.
   Ⓒ burning methane.
   Ⓓ melting plastic.

2. The word **converted** means
   Ⓐ changed.
   Ⓑ lost.
   Ⓒ increased.
   Ⓓ decreased.

3. In the Amtrak derailment of July 2002, what happened second?
   Ⓐ The sun heated the metal rails.
   Ⓑ The track bent several inches.
   Ⓒ The train's wheels left the rails.
   Ⓓ The atoms in the rails moved rapidly.

4. Which of these objects conducts heat most rapidly?
   Ⓐ dry cloth
   Ⓑ metal
   Ⓒ plastic
   Ⓓ wood

5. If your home is heated with an 85-percent-efficient furnace, how much energy is lost?
   Ⓐ 5 percent
   Ⓑ 10 percent
   Ⓒ 15 percent
   Ⓓ 85 percent

6. An inefficient truck
   Ⓐ gets a lot of miles out of each gallon of gas.
   Ⓑ gets few miles out of each gallon of gas.
   Ⓒ does not have a muffler.
   Ⓓ has a hot engine after running.

Dr. Ruth Patrick, Water Pioneer

Dr. Ruth Patrick was born in 1907. Her dad took her on walks. They picked up things and took them home. Then, they looked at them with a microscope. Ruth loved nature. When she grew up, she went to college. She went for eight years. She earned a doctoral degree in science. Back then, few women went to college. Even fewer became doctors.

Ruth got married and had a son. At that time, women with children did not work. So she **volunteered** at the Academy of Natural Sciences. This means that she worked for no pay. She took care of the museum's slide collection. Ruth looked at the slides and thought about them. Soon, she started a new field of science called limnology. It is the study of fresh water.

One day, Ruth gave a talk. A man who ran a company heard Ruth speak and hired her. He told her to find a way to measure water pollution. No one had ever done this. She had to think of how to do it. So Ruth gathered diatoms. They are algae. They have just one cell. Water animals eat them. The amount of diatoms shows how clean water is. To get them, Ruth invented a box. First, it was put in the water. Then, it was hooked to the bottom. A cork kept it afloat. As water went through it, diatoms stuck to glass slides. She removed the slides and studied them.

Ruth worried about water quality twenty years before pollution was talked about. Later, Ruth showed that the Great Salt Lake in Utah used to be fresh water that turned salty. How? Sun and wind made the lake's water evaporate. This means that it changed into water vapor. The water left behind got saltier. Ruth was one of the first scientists to discover acid rain. Smoke rises into clouds. It makes the water drops in the clouds dirty. Then, acid rain falls.

Ruth taught at a college for thirty-five years. She was the first woman to be chair of the board of the Academy of Natural Sciences. In 1996, she won the National Medal of Science. It is an award given to those who have added new ideas to science.

Dr. Ruth Patrick

Ruth lived to be more than 101 years old. Scientists still use her methods. They keep track of the amount of diatoms in fresh water. They want to keep water free of pollution.

Dr. Ruth Patrick, Water Pioneer

Dr. Ruth Patrick was born in 1907. As a child, her dad took her on nature walks. They picked up things and brought them home to look at under a microscope. When Ruth grew up, she went to college for eight years and earned a doctoral degree in science. Back then, few women went to college. Very few became doctors.

Ruth got married and had a son. At that time, women with children did not work. So she worked without pay. She **volunteered** at the Academy of Natural Sciences. She took care of the museum's slide collection. Ruth looked at the slides and thought about them. She started a new branch of science called limnology. It is the study of fresh water.

One day, Ruth gave a talk. A man who ran a company heard her speak and hired her to think of some way to measure water pollution. Ruth was the first person to ever do this. She collected diatoms, one-celled algae that provide food for water animals. The amount of diatoms in water is linked to its quality. To get them, Ruth had to invent a device. First, she placed a box in the water. Then, she anchored it to the bottom. A cork kept it floating. As the water flowed through it, diatoms stuck to glass slides. Ruth removed and studied these slides.

Ruth worried about water quality twenty years before "pollution" was a household word. Later, she proved that the Great Salt Lake in Utah was once fresh water that became salty. How? The sun and wind caused the lake's water to evaporate. It changed into water vapor. The water left behind got saltier. Ruth was one of the first scientists to discover acid rain. Air pollution dirties the water droplets within clouds. Then, dirty water falls as rain. Acid rain is bad for lakes and forests.

Dr. Ruth Patrick

Ruth taught at a college for thirty-five years. She was the first woman to be chair of the board of the Academy of Natural Sciences. In 1996, she won the National Medal of Science. It is a major honor. It goes to those who have added new ideas to science.

Ruth lived to be more than 101 years old. Scientists still use her methods to keep track of diatoms. They analyze the kinds and amounts. It is the best way to measure water quality. Then, steps can be taken to prevent water pollution from getting worse.

Dr. Ruth Patrick, Water Pioneer

Dr. Ruth Patrick was born in 1907. As a child, her dad took her on nature walks every week. They picked up things and brought them home to look at under a microscope. Nature fascinated Ruth. When she grew up, she went to college for eight years and earned a doctoral degree in science. Back then, few women went to college, and even fewer became doctors.

Ruth got married and had a son. At that time, women with children did not work, so she worked without pay. She **volunteered** at the Academy of Natural Sciences, taking care of the museum's slide collection. Ruth looked at the slides and thought about them. Eventually, she started a new branch of science called limnology. It is the study of fresh water.

One day, Ruth gave a talk, and an executive who ran a company heard her speak. He was so impressed by her that he hired her to think of some way to measure water pollution. Ruth was the first person to ever do this. She decided the best way to do it was to collect diatoms, one-celled algae that provide food for water animals. The amount of diatoms is linked to water quality. To gather them, Ruth had to invent a device. First, she placed a box in the water and anchored it to the bottom. A cork kept it floating. Then, as the water flowed through it, diatoms stuck to glass slides. Ruth removed and studied these slides carefully.

What Ruth saw in the water worried her. In fact, she was concerned about water quality twenty years before "pollution" was a household word. Later, she proved that the Great Salt Lake in Utah was once fresh water that became salty over time. How? The sun and wind caused the lake's water to evaporate. It changed into water vapor, and the water left behind got saltier. Ruth was one of the first scientists to discover acid rain, which damages lakes and forests. Air pollution dirties the water droplets within clouds. Then, the dirty water falls as acid rain.

Dr. Ruth Patrick

Ruth taught at a college for thirty-five years. She was the first woman to be chair of the board of the Academy of Natural Sciences. In 1996, she won the National Medal of Science. This major honor goes to those who have added new ideas to science.

Ruth lived to be more than 101 years old. Scientists still use her methods to collect diatoms. They analyze the kinds and amounts. It is the best way to measure water quality. Then, steps can be taken to prevent water pollution from getting worse.

Dr. Ruth Patrick, Water Pioneer

Directions: Darken the best answer choice.

1. In order to determine how dirty water was, Ruth studied
   - Ⓐ how many particles of dirt were floating in the water.
   - Ⓑ the amount of salt in the water.
   - Ⓒ how fast water evaporated in the sunlight.
   - Ⓓ single-celled organisms called diatoms.

2. The word **volunteered** means
   - Ⓐ started advertising.
   - Ⓑ brought in donations (money).
   - Ⓒ did work for free.
   - Ⓓ took over the organization.

3. Which of these events occurred third?
   - Ⓐ Ruth volunteered at the Academy of Natural Sciences.
   - Ⓑ Ruth designed a way to measure the level of pollution in water.
   - Ⓒ Ruth won the National Medal of Science.
   - Ⓓ Ruth earned a doctoral degree in science.

4. You can tell that Ruth was interested in
   - Ⓐ understanding rivers, lakes, and streams.
   - Ⓑ earning a lot of money.
   - Ⓒ understanding the oceans.
   - Ⓓ exploring mountain ranges.

5. Ruth did not make advances in our scientific knowledge of
   - Ⓐ acid rain.
   - Ⓑ how fresh water lakes become salty.
   - Ⓒ limnology.
   - Ⓓ the bleaching of coral reefs in the sea.

6. In the Adirondack Mountains, some lakes have become acidic. Why?
   - Ⓐ Sun and pollution caused a lot of the lakes' water to evaporate, and the water left behind became acidic.
   - Ⓑ Factories put smoke into the air, and wind blew it to the Adirondacks. Raindrops formed around the dirt particles and fell into these lakes.
   - Ⓒ Ruth's methods of measuring water pollution in these lakes caused them to become acidic.
   - Ⓓ The Academy of Natural Sciences conducted experiments that accidentally made these lakes become acidic.

Bill Gates, Inventor and Humanitarian

Have you ever played on an Xbox 360®? If so, thank Bill Gates. His company invented it. Bill was born in 1955. Back then, computers were huge. It took a whole building to house one! And they cost a lot. Just the government and a few colleges had them. But Bill went to a school that had access to a computer by phone lines. The computer thrilled Bill and his friend, Paul Allen. When Bill was in eleventh grade, a company hired the boys. They fixed its software (programs). They were "paid" with free time on the computer.

The teens graduated. Then, they went to college. Neither one finished. They dropped out. They formed a company. Its name is Microsoft®. Their company wrote programs to make computers do math or word processing. They worked hard to make computers user-friendly. Their programs changed the world and helped to put computers in most American homes.

Bill Gates

It all began in 1975. Bill and Paul saw an ad. It was for a computer called the Altair®. It was almost useless. There was no real way for a user to tell it what to do! So Bill did something crazy. He called Altair's makers. He told them that he had a BASIC® program. It could tell the Altair what to do. Bill did not even own an Altair! And he didn't have the program. The company asked to see his product. So Bill worked night and day for a month. At last, he had the program ready. Paul took it to the company. Bill and Paul didn't even know if it would work. But it did work—perfectly.

The pair left college. They got to work. Major companies asked for their help. Everyone saw that computers were the wave of the future. Yet few people knew how to make them do things. One big company, IBM®, came to Microsoft and asked for an operating system for its computers. Bill bought another company's operating system for $50,000. He modified it and had IBM put it on their machines. Each time a machine sold, Bill got part of the profits. He made millions of dollars in the first year. His program, named MS-DOS®, became the operating system for most computers. Later, Microsoft invented Windows® and then Internet Explorer®. It created Word®, Excel®, and PowerPoint®. Many of the programs you use on the computer came from Microsoft.

In 1983, Paul Allen had cancer. He left the company. He got better. The men are still friends. In 1994, Bill got married. Now, he has three children. He stopped doing the day-to-day running of Microsoft in 2000. He became the chairman of the board. In 2008, he let go of more control. He wanted to spend more time with his family and do charity work. Since Bill owns a lot of the company's stock, he still has a major say in the things that go on.

By the age of thirty-three, Bill was a billionaire. He is one of the richest men on Earth. He and his wife want to share their wealth. They plan to give away 98 percent of it. They formed the Bill and Melinda Gates Foundation in 2000. It gives money to **charities**. It tries to improve people's health and education. One of its goals is to give children vaccines. This will keep them from dying.

Bill Gates, Inventor and Humanitarian

Have you ever played on an Xbox 360®? If so, you can thank Bill Gates. His company invented it. Bill was born in 1955. Back then, computers were huge. It took a building to house one! And they cost so much that only the government and a few colleges had them. Bill's parents put him in a school that had access to a computer through phone lines. The computer fascinated Bill and his friend, Paul Allen. When Bill was in eleventh grade, a company hired the boys to fix its software (programs). They were "paid" with free time on the computer.

After the teens graduated, they went to college. However, neither one finished. They dropped out to form a company. Its name is Microsoft®. Their company wrote programs to make computers do tasks, such as word processing or math problems. They worked hard to make computers user-friendly. Their programs changed the world and helped to put computers in most American homes.

Bill Gates

It all began in 1975. Bill and Paul saw an ad selling a computer called the Altair®. There was no real way for a user to tell it what to do! So Bill did something crazy. He called Altair's makers and told them that he had a BASIC® program. It could tell the Altair what to do. Bill did not even own an Altair! He didn't have the program, either. But the company asked to see his product. So Bill worked night and day for a month. At last, he had the program ready. Paul took it to the company. Bill and Paul didn't even know if it would work. But it did work—perfectly.

The pair left college and got to work. Major companies asked for their help. Everyone saw that computers were the wave of the future. Few people knew how to make them do things. IBM®, a big company, came to Microsoft and asked for an operating system for its computers. Bill bought another company's operating system for $50,000. Then, he modified it and had IBM put it on their machines. Each time a machine sold, Bill got part of the profits. He made millions of dollars in the first year. His program, named MS-DOS®, became the operating system for most computers. Later, Microsoft invented Windows® and then Internet Explorer®. It created Word®, Excel®, and PowerPoint®. Many of the programs you use on the computer came from Microsoft.

In 1983, Paul Allen left the company. He had cancer and didn't want to work anymore. He made a full recovery, and the men remain friends. In 1994, Bill got married. Now, he has three children. He stepped down from the day-to-day running of Microsoft in 2000. He took the position of chairman of the board. In 2008, he let go of more control. He wanted to spend more time with his family and do charity work. However, since Bill owns a lot of the company's stock, he still has a major say in the things that go on.

Bill Gates was a billionaire by the time he was thirty-three. Today, he is one of the richest men on Earth. He and his wife want to share their riches. They plan to give away 98 percent of their wealth. They formed the Bill and Melinda Gates Foundation in 2000. It gives money to **charities**. It focuses on helping to improve people's health and education. One of its top goals is to vaccinate children around the world. This will keep them from dying due to disease.

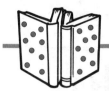

Bill Gates, Inventor and Humanitarian

Have you ever played on an Xbox 360®? If so, you can thank Bill Gates because his company invented it. Bill was born in October 1955. Back then, computers were so huge that it took a building to house one. Also, they cost so much that only the government and a few colleges had them. Bill's parents put him in a school that had access to a computer through phone lines. The computer fascinated Bill and his friend, Paul Allen. When Bill was in eleventh grade, a company asked the boys to fix its software (programs) in exchange for free time on the computer.

Bill and Paul went to college, but neither one finished. They dropped out to form a company named Microsoft®. Their company wrote programs to make computers do tasks, such as word processing or math calculations. They worked hard to make computers user-friendly. Their programs changed the world and helped to put computers in most American homes.

Bill Gates

It all began in January 1975. Bill and Paul saw an ad selling the Altair® computer. Since there was no real way for a user to tell it what to do, it was almost useless. So Bill did something crazy: he called Altair's makers and told them that he had a BASIC® program that could tell the Altair what to do. Bill did not own an Altair or have any such program! The company asked to see his product. So Bill worked night and day for a month until he had the program ready. Paul took it to the company. Bill and Paul didn't even know if it would work. But it did work—perfectly.

The pair left college and got to work. Major companies asked for their help. Everyone saw that computers were the wave of the future, but few people knew how to make them do things. IBM®, a large company, came to Microsoft and asked for an operating system for its computers. Bill bought another company's operating system for $50,000, modified it, and had IBM put it on their machines. Each time a machine sold, Bill got part of the profits. He made millions of dollars in the first year. His program, named MS-DOS®, became the operating system for most computers. Later, Microsoft invented Windows® and Internet Explorer®. It created Word®, Excel®, and PowerPoint®. Many of the programs you use on the computer came from Microsoft.

In 1983, Paul Allen left the company because he had cancer. He made a full recovery, and the men remain friends. In 1994, Bill got married. Now, he has three children. He stepped down from the day-to-day running of Microsoft in 2000 and became chairman of the board. In 2008, he let go of more control. He wanted to spend more time with his family and do charity work. However, since Bill owns a lot of the company's stock, he still has a major say in the things that go on.

Bill Gates was a billionaire by the time he was thirty-three. Today, he is one of the richest men on Earth. He and his wife want to share their riches. They intend to give away 98 percent of their wealth. They formed the Bill and Melinda Gates Foundation in 2000 to give money to **charities**. It focuses on helping to improve people's health and education. One of its top goals is to vaccinate children around the world to protect them from disease.

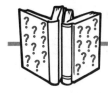

Bill Gates, Inventor and Humanitarian

Directions: Darken the best answer choice.

1. Bill Gates and Paul Allen invented the
   - (A) first computer.
   - (B) Altair® computer.
   - (C) Windows® operating system.
   - (D) Internet.

2. The word **charities** means
   - (A) new computer companies.
   - (B) children's hospitals.
   - (C) colleges.
   - (D) groups that help people in need.

3. Which event occurred second?
   - (A) Bill created the MS-DOS® operating system.
   - (B) Bill started his own company.
   - (C) Bill became a billionaire.
   - (D) Bill and his wife set up a foundation to help good causes.

4. Microsoft® did *not* invent the
   - (A) software program called PowerPoint®.
   - (B) Google™ search engine.
   - (C) Internet Explorer® search engine.
   - (D) Xbox 360®.

5. Think about Bill and the Altair computer. You can tell that he is
   - (A) impatient.
   - (B) shy.
   - (C) bold.
   - (D) quiet.

6. Bill Gates changed the world because he
   - (A) designed software that let average people use computers.
   - (B) made computers much smaller.
   - (C) set up a program to teach all American children to use a computer.
   - (D) funded the research that found the cure for cancer.

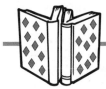

Sinkholes

You know about the physical weathering of stones and soil. It is due to wind and moving water or ice. The wind and water slowly wear away the rocks and dirt. Did you know that there is chemical weathering, too? Rain falls. Water trickles down through the grass and soil. It picks up carbon from rotting plant matter. The plant matter could be dead trees. It may be fallen leaves. The carbon makes the water more acidic. It drips into little cracks and holes. It seeps down to an underground rock layer. Millions of years pass. Billions of rainstorms happen. The acid water dissolves the rock. The cracks and holes get bigger. They turn into underground tunnels and rooms. They become limestone caverns. Some of these caves have huge rooms and tunnels. People go into them. Others have deep, thin passages. No one can enter. Scientists think that there may be 50,000 of these caverns beneath the United States. The most famous of these is Mammoth Cave. It is in Kentucky. It is the longest cave system in the world. Its tunnels are miles long. The cave system is a national park. In the southern part of the park lies a large sinkhole. It is called "Cedar Sink."

What is a sinkhole? It is a depression in the ground. It often forms when a cave roof falls in. Another cause is when people pump out groundwater faster than rain and melting snow can replace it. A sinkhole may form slowly. It may form suddenly. When one forms suddenly, it can be a danger. In 1981, this happened in Winter Park, Florida. Mae Rose Owens was in her backyard  with her dog. To her shock, a huge tree nearby suddenly vanished! And it didn't fall over as if it had been cut down. Mae saw that more trees were disappearing. She took her dog and fled. It's a good thing she did. The sinkhole kept growing for twenty-four hours. In the end, it swallowed her house, five cars, and part of a car repair shop. A pickup truck, an in-ground swimming pool, and numerous trees and bushes were gone, too.

There are sinkholes all over the world. In the United States, they are most common in Florida and other southern states. In Alabama, more than 4,000 sinkholes formed in the past one hundred years. Scientists know places where they are apt to form. But they cannot tell when one will form.

Sinkholes have helped scientists to know which parts of the ocean floor were once land. During the last Ice Age, much of the water in the seas turned into ice. The level of the oceans fell. More land was **exposed**. When the Ice Age ended, Earth warmed up. The ice melted. The water level rose. Water covered the land. This is what happened in an area of "blue holes" near the Bahamas. These are deep, dark holes in the sea's floor. Some are hundreds of feet deep. They were once sinkholes on land. They formed about 18,000 years ago. They formed in the same way that all sinkholes and limestone caverns form. Divers like these holes. But they can be deadly. There are strong currents. They can suck a diver down. This makes it hard to get back to the surface. Only twice a day can the holes be explored safely. Both times are at low tide.

Sinkholes

You know about the physical weathering of stones and soil due to wind and moving water or ice. The wind and water slowly wear away the rocks and dirt. But did you know that there is chemical weathering, too? When rain falls, water trickles down through the grass and soil. It picks up carbon from rotting plant matter. The plant matter may be dead trees or fallen leaves. The carbon makes the water more acidic. It drips into little cracks and holes. At last, it seeps down to an underground rock layer. Over millions of years and billions of rainstorms, the acid water dissolves the rock. The cracks and holes grow bigger. They become the underground tunnels and rooms known as limestone caverns. Some of these caves have huge rooms and tunnels that can hold many people. Others have deep, narrow passages that no one can enter. Scientists think that there are about 50,000 of these caverns beneath the United States. Perhaps the most famous of these is Mammoth Cave in Kentucky. It is the longest cave system in the world. Its tunnels are miles long. The cave system is a national park. In the southern part of the park lies a large sinkhole. It is called "Cedar Sink."

Just what is a sinkhole? It is a depression in the ground. It is often caused by a cave roof falling in. Another cause is when people pump out groundwater faster than rain and melting snow can replace it. A sinkhole may form slowly or suddenly. When one forms suddenly, it can be a danger. In 1981, one formed suddenly in Winter Park, Florida. Mae Rose Owens was in her

backyard with her dog. To her shock, a huge tree nearby suddenly vanished! And it didn't fall over as if it had been cut down. Mae noticed that more trees were disappearing. She took her dog and fled. It's a good thing she did. The sinkhole kept growing for twenty-four hours. In the end, it swallowed her house, five cars, part of a car repair shop, a pickup truck, an in-ground swimming pool, and numerous trees and bushes.

There are sinkholes all over the world. In the United States, they are most common in Florida and other southern states. In Alabama, more than 4,000 sinkholes formed in the past one hundred years. Scientists know places where sinkholes are apt to form, but they cannot predict when they will form.

Sinkholes have been important in helping scientists to identify which parts of the ocean floor were once land. During the last Ice Age, much of the water in the seas was trapped in ice. The level of the oceans fell. More land was **exposed**. When the Ice Age ended, the ice melted. The water level rose. Now that land may be many feet under the water. This is what happened in an area of "blue holes" near the Bahamas. These are deep, dark holes in the sea's floor. Some are hundreds of feet deep. They were once sinkholes on land. They formed about 18,000 years ago in the same way that all sinkholes and limestone caverns form. These holes fascinate divers. But they can be deadly. Strong currents can suck a diver down. This makes it hard to fight one's way to the surface. Only twice a day at low tide can the holes be explored safely.

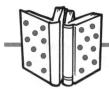

Sinkholes

You know about the physical weathering of rocks and dirt from the action of wind and moving water or ice. The wind and water wear away the rocks and dirt. But did you know that there is chemical weathering, too? When rain falls, water trickles down through the grass and soil. The water picks up carbon from rotting plant matter such as dead trees or fallen leaves. The carbon makes the water more acidic as it drips into little cracks and holes and seeps down to an underground rock layer. Over millions of years and billions of rainstorms, the acid water dissolves the rock. The cracks and holes grow bigger and bigger. They become the underground tunnels and rooms known as limestone caverns. Some of these caves have gigantic rooms and tunnels that can hold many people. Others have deep, narrow passages that no one can enter. Scientists think that there may be 50,000 caverns beneath the United States. Yet very few have been found. Perhaps the most famous of these is Mammoth Cave in Kentucky, the longest cave system in the world. The cave system is a national park. In the southern part of the park lies a huge sinkhole called "Cedar Sink."

Just what is a sinkhole? A sinkhole is a depression in the ground, usually caused by a cave roof collapse. Another cause is when people pump out groundwater faster than rain and melting snow can replace it. A sinkhole may form slowly or suddenly. When one forms suddenly, it can be dangerous. In 1981, in Winter Park, Florida, Mae Rose Owens was in her backyard with her dog. To her shock, a huge tree suddenly vanished! And it didn't fall over as if someone had chopped it down. She noticed that more trees were disappearing. She took her dog and fled. It's a good thing she did. The sinkhole kept growing for twenty-four hours. By the time it was done, it had swallowed her house, five cars, part of a car repair shop, a pickup truck, an in-ground swimming pool, and numerous trees and bushes.

There are sinkholes all over the world. In the United States, they are most common in Florida and other southern states. In Alabama, more than 4,000 sinkholes appeared in the past one hundred years. Although scientists know places where sinkholes are apt to form, they cannot predict when they will form.

Sinkholes have been important in helping scientists to identify which parts of the ocean floor were once land. During the last Ice Age, much of the water in the seas was trapped in ice. This means that the level of the oceans fell. More land was **exposed**. When the Ice Age ended and the ice melted, the water level rose. Today, that land may be many feet under the water. This happened in an area of "blue holes" near the Bahamas. These are deep, dark holes in the ocean's floor. Some of them are hundreds of feet deep. These sinkholes formed on land about 18,000 years ago in the same way that all sinkholes and limestone caverns form. Although these holes fascinate divers, they can be deadly. Strong currents can suck a diver down, making it almost impossible to fight one's way to the surface. Only twice a day at low tide can these holes be explored safely.

Sinkholes

Directions: Darken the best answer choice.

1. Where is Cedar Sink located?
   - Ⓐ the Bahamas
   - Ⓑ Kentucky
   - Ⓒ Florida
   - Ⓓ Alabama

2. The word **exposed** means
   - Ⓐ raised.
   - Ⓑ lowered.
   - Ⓒ destroyed.
   - Ⓓ uncovered.

3. Which event occurred first?
   - Ⓐ Sinkholes were on the seafloor.
   - Ⓑ Sea levels rose.
   - Ⓒ The last Ice Age began.
   - Ⓓ Sea levels dropped.

4. A sinkhole may form as the result of
   - Ⓐ a major flood.
   - Ⓑ an explosion.
   - Ⓒ removing groundwater.
   - Ⓓ building a dam.

5. A *cavern* is to a *sinkhole* as a *building* is to a
   - Ⓐ *sudden tornado.*
   - Ⓑ *roof collapse.*
   - Ⓒ *new addition.*
   - Ⓓ *coal mine.*

6. A sinkhole would be most likely to form in the state of
   - Ⓐ Georgia.
   - Ⓑ New York.
   - Ⓒ Alaska.
   - Ⓓ Wisconsin.

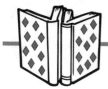

The Legacy of Turkey Red Wheat

Don't ever think that you're too young to make a difference. Russian children about your age changed U.S. history. The children were Mennonites. This Christian group started out in Holland. Mennonites did not believe in war. They would not fight in the army. As a result, people did not like them. So they left Holland. First, they fled to Prussia. Then, in 1790, they went to Russia. That's when Catherine the Great offered them a deal. They did not have to be soldiers and could follow their religion. In Russia, the Mennonites were great farmers. They planted Turkey Red wheat. This winter wheat came from Turkey. It was planted in the fall. (Most wheat is planted in the spring.) The Turkey Red wheat plants died in the winter. But the roots stayed alive. In the spring, the wheat sprouted again. It started growing weeks before spring wheat could be planted.

By 1871, the leader of Russia had changed. The Mennonites were told they must join the troops. They chose to leave. They went to Kansas. Why? There were thousands of acres available. Plus, the U.S. had a law. It let people avoid the army for religious reasons. The Mennonites could not take much with them. Their most important possession was Turkey Red wheat. So parents had their children choose two gallons of wheat. They picked it one grain at a time! (A grain of wheat is about the same size as an uncooked popcorn kernel.) The children looked at each grain. They chose just the best ones. In America, the immigrants would have no way to get more of the seed. Two gallons was about 250,000 grains. Think of how tiring that job must have been!

In 1874, the Mennonites came to Kansas. That fall, they planted the wheat grains their children had chosen. Their neighbors thought they were crazy. The settlers already living in Kansas had had bad luck with wheat. They planted spring wheat. It did not live through the harsh, dry summers. They thought that wheat was the wrong crop for Kansas. And they had never tried planting in the fall.

The neighbors had to reconsider what they knew about wheat once they saw that first **bountiful** harvest of Turkey Red wheat. In those days, news moved slowly. There were miles between farms on the prairie. Just people living in the immediate area of the Mennonites knew about the success of the winter wheat. It took almost another twenty-five years before most of the farmers in the state started to grow Turkey Red wheat.

Turkey Red wheat helped to make the American Midwest into the "Breadbasket of the World." Now, newer, better kinds of wheat are grown. They are based on Turkey Red wheat. Each year, U.S. farmers grow hundreds of millions of bushels of wheat. More is grown in Kansas than any other state. It is called the "Granary of the Nation." Turkey Red wheat is a legacy. That means it is a gift handed down over time. This gift came from children. Their small hands chose the seeds.

The Legacy of Turkey Red Wheat

Don't ever think that you're too young to have an impact on the world. Russian children about your age changed the course of American history. The children were Mennonites. This Christian group started out in Holland. Mennonites did not believe in war. They would not serve in the army. This made them unpopular. First, they fled to Prussia. Then, in 1790, they moved to Russia. That's when Catherine the Great offered them religious freedom and freedom from being in the troops. In Russia, the Mennonites became successful farmers. They planted Turkey Red wheat. This winter wheat came from Turkey. Unlike other kinds of wheat, it was planted in the fall. (Other kinds were planted in the spring.) The Turkey Red wheat plants died during the harsh winter. But the root system stayed alive. In the spring, this wheat sprouted. It started weeks before spring wheat could even be planted.

By 1871, the leader of Russia had changed. The Mennonites were told they had to join the service. Instead, they went to Kansas. There were thousands of acres available. Plus, the U.S. had a law. It let people avoid military service for religious reasons. Before the Mennonites emigrated, they found out that they couldn't take much with them. They knew that their most important possession was Turkey Red wheat. So parents had their children select two gallons of red wheat. They picked it out one grain at a time! (A grain of wheat is about the same size as an uncooked popcorn kernel.) The children looked at each grain closely. They were to bring only the most perfect ones. Once the immigrants got to America, there would be no way to get more of the precious wheat seed. Two gallons was about 250,000 grains. Think of how tiring that task must have been!

In 1874, the Mennonites arrived in Kansas. That fall, they planted the wheat grains their children had chosen so carefully. Their neighbors thought they were crazy. The settlers already living in Kansas had had bad luck growing wheat. They only had spring wheat. It rarely survived through the harsh, dry summers. Not only was wheat considered the wrong crop for Kansas, but planting in the fall had never been tried before.

The neighbors had to reconsider what they knew about growing wheat once they saw that first **bountiful** harvest of Turkey Red wheat. Yet, in those days, news moved slowly. And there were miles between farms on the prairie. Only people living in the immediate area of the Mennonites saw that they should plant the winter wheat. It took almost another twenty-five years before the majority of the farmers in the state began growing Turkey Red wheat.

Turkey Red wheat helped to make the American Midwest into the "Breadbasket of the World." Today, newer, even better kinds of wheat are grown. They are based on Turkey Red wheat. Each year, U.S. farmers harvest hundreds of millions of bushels of wheat. More is grown in Kansas than in any other state. That's why it is called the "Granary of the Nation." Turkey Red wheat is a legacy. That means it is a gift handed down over time. And this gift came from the little hands of children. They chose the seeds.

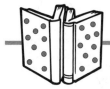

The Legacy of Turkey Red Wheat

Don't ever think that you're too young to have an impact on the world. Russian children about your age changed the course of American history. The children were Mennonites. This Christian group originated in Holland. Mennonites did not believe in war and refused to serve in the army. This made them unpopular. First, they fled to Prussia. Then, in 1790, they moved to Russia when Catherine the Great offered them religious freedom and the ability to stay out of the military. In Russia, the Mennonites became successful farmers. They planted Turkey Red wheat. This winter wheat came from Turkey. Unlike other types of wheat, it was planted in the fall. (Other kinds were planted in the spring.) The actual plants died during the harsh winter. But the root system survived. In the spring, this wheat sprouted weeks before spring wheat could even be planted.

By 1871, leadership in Russia had changed. The Mennonites were told they had to join the troops. Instead, they moved to Kansas. There were thousands of acres available, and the U.S. had a law that let people avoid military service for religious reasons. Before the Mennonites emigrated, they found out that they couldn't take much with them. They knew that their most important possession was Turkey Red wheat. So parents had their children choose two gallons of red wheat, one grain at a time! (A grain of wheat is about the same size as an uncooked popcorn kernel.) The children examined each grain closely. They were to bring only the most perfect seeds. Once the immigrants arrived in America, there would be no way to get more of the precious wheat seed. Two gallons was about 250,000 individual grains. Think of how exhausting that task must have been!

In 1874, the Mennonites arrived in Kansas. That fall, they planted the wheat grains their children had chosen so carefully. Their neighbors thought they were crazy. The settlers already living in Kansas had had very poor luck growing wheat. They only had spring wheat. It rarely survived the harsh, dry conditions of summer. Not only was wheat considered the wrong crop for Kansas, but planting in the fall had never been tried before.

The neighbors had to reconsider what they knew about growing wheat once they saw that first **bountiful** harvest of Turkey Red wheat. Yet, in those days, news moved slowly, and there were miles between farms on the prairie. Only people living in the immediate area of the Mennonites realized that they should plant the winter wheat. It took almost another twenty-five years before the majority of the farmers in the state switched over to Turkey Red wheat.

Turkey Red wheat helped to make the American Midwest into the "Breadbasket of the World." Today, even better strains of wheat are grown. They are based on Turkey Red wheat. Every year, U.S. farmers harvest hundreds of millions of bushels of wheat. Since more is grown in the state of Kansas than in any other state, it is called the "Granary of the Nation." Turkey Red wheat is a legacy—a gift handed down over time. And this gift came from the little hands of the children who chose the seeds.

The Legacy of Turkey Red Wheat

Directions: Darken the best answer choice.

1. Turkey Red wheat was planted in the
   - Ⓐ spring.
   - Ⓑ summer.
   - Ⓒ fall.
   - Ⓓ winter.

2. The word **bountiful** means
   - Ⓐ small.
   - Ⓑ expected.
   - Ⓒ large.
   - Ⓓ strange.

3. Where was the third place that the Mennonites lived?
   - Ⓐ Prussia
   - Ⓑ the United States
   - Ⓒ Holland
   - Ⓓ Russia

4. One grain of Turkey Red wheat is about the same size as a(n)
   - Ⓐ uncooked popcorn kernel.
   - Ⓑ pinhead.
   - Ⓒ strawberry.
   - Ⓓ walnut.

5. The Mennonites moved around because they
   - Ⓐ wanted to teach people how to grow wheat.
   - Ⓑ did not want to be soldiers.
   - Ⓒ wanted a place to plant Turkey Red wheat.
   - Ⓓ had trouble learning new languages.

6. Turkey Red wheat came to America by
   - Ⓐ ship.
   - Ⓑ plane.
   - Ⓒ train.
   - Ⓓ blimp.

People Affect Water

Humans have always needed water. That is why cities and towns began along rivers. Over time, people found out that pools of water lie underground. This water storage is called an aquifer. So, in many places, people drilled down through the dirt. They pumped up the groundwater. The amount of groundwater is called the water table.

The water in an aquifer gets refilled by rain or melting snow. But what if more water gets removed than flows back in? The water table drops. This is bad news. As the water table falls, the land above it may crack and sink. The land may cave in. This can harm roads and buildings. It has already happened in Arizona and other places where people are using the groundwater too fast. And aquifers near cities can be polluted. How? Sewers may leak. Chemicals may seep from trash dumps. Road runoff and fertilizers can cause trouble, too. Anything—such as weed killer—put on the ground may find its way into an aquifer.

Many people do not find wetlands pretty. Yet they are important. Marshes and swamps help refill aquifers. Plus, they can store water. This cuts down on flooding after a heavy rain. People have wrecked more than half of the wetlands that were once in the United States.* There used to be 215 million acres. Now, parts of San Francisco and Boston stand on former wetlands. The swampy land was filled in. Trucks dumped loads of dirt. This built up the land. It became dry. Then, people put buildings and streets on it. This happens in other places, too. A whole nation called the Netherlands stands on land reclaimed from the sea.

Tidal marshes are a type of wetland. In these places, fresh and salt water mix. Every twelve hours, a tidal marsh fills or empties. It is based on the rise and fall of the tides. These marshes are home to a lot of animals, and the water grasses remove **pollutants**. But many tidal marshes have been ruined. People have built homes along the coast. In the United States, more than half of the tidal marshes are gone.

A bioswale is a kind of landscaping. It is planted in order to keep pollutants out of water. One type of bioswale is a planted area in or around a parking lot. The planted area replaces storm drains. How does it work? Rain falls or snow melts on the parking lot. The water runs off the pavement into the soil. It will soak down until it reaches an aquifer. Soil and plant roots in the bioswale trap toxins. (Think of the dirt a parking lot might have: gas, oil, and pieces of metal or rubber.) Over time, bacteria in the dirt break down these things. They change the chemical form of the toxins. They become harmless.

*This does not include Alaska.

People Affect Water

Humans have always needed fresh water. That's why civilizations sprang up along rivers. Over time, people found that there is water stored underground. They could pump this water to the surface. So, in many places, people drilled down through the soil to reach aquifers. These are pools of groundwater. The amount of groundwater is called the water table.

If more water is taken from the aquifer than is replaced by rain or melting snow, the water table drops. This is bad news. As the water table falls, the land above it may crack and sink. The land may cave in. This can damage roads and buildings. This has already happened in Arizona and other places where people are using the groundwater too fast. In addition, aquifers near cities can be polluted. How? Sewers may leak. Chemicals may flow into the ground from trash dumps. Road runoff and farm fertilizers can get into an aquifer and cause problems, too. Any chemical—such as weed killer—applied to the ground may find its way into an aquifer.

Many people do not find wetlands beautiful. Yet they are important. Marshes and swamps refill aquifers. Plus, they store water. This cuts down on flooding after a heavy rain. People have wrecked more than half of the 215 million acres of wetlands that the United States* once had. Now, parts of some cities, such as San Francisco and Boston, stand on former wetlands. Trucks dumped dirt. This built up the swampy land. It became dry. Then, people put buildings and streets on the new land. The whole nation called the Netherlands stands on land reclaimed from the sea.

Tidal marshes are a type of wetland. In these places, fresh and salt water mix. Every twelve hours, salt water will fill or empty a tidal marsh. This comes from the rise and fall of the tides. These marshes provide a home for many animals, and the aquatic grasses filter out **pollutants**. But coastal development has ruined many tidal marshes. More than half have been done away with in the United States.

A bioswale is a kind of landscaping. It is meant to keep pollutants from getting into water. One type of bioswale is a planted area within or around a parking lot. The planted area replaces storm drains. How does it work? Rain falls or snow melts on the parking lot. The water runs off the pavement and into the soil. It will soak down into the soil until it reaches an aquifer. But first the soil and plant roots in the bioswale trap toxins. These are things such as gas, oil, and pieces of metal or rubber. Over time, bacteria in the dirt break down these particles. They change the chemical form and make the toxins harmless.

*This does not include Alaska.

People Affect Water

Humans have always needed a supply of fresh water. That's why all civilizations—and most cities—sprang up along rivers. Over time, people found that there is water stored underground. They could pump this water to the surface. In many places, people drilled down through the soil to reach these aquifers. The amount of groundwater is called the water table.

Rain and melting snow refill aquifers. But when more water is taken out than is replaced, the water table drops. As the water table falls, the land above may crack and sink. The land may cave in, damaging roads and buildings. This has already happened in Arizona and other places where people are using the groundwater too fast. In addition, aquifers near cities may be polluted. Sewers may leak. Chemicals may flow into the ground from trash dumps. Road runoff and farm fertilizers can get into an aquifer and cause problems, too.

Many people do not find wetlands beautiful, but they are important. Marshes and swamps help to refill aquifers. They also store water, which cuts down on the flooding a heavy rain can cause. Yet people have destroyed more than half of the 215 million acres of wetlands that were once in the United States.* Parts of some cities, including San Francisco and Boston, stand on former wetlands. The swampy land was filled in with truckloads of dirt. Then, people put buildings and streets on the new land. The whole nation called the Netherlands stands on land reclaimed from the sea.

Tidal marshes are places where fresh and salt water mix. Every twelve hours, salt water will fill or empty a tidal marsh with the rise and fall of the tides. These places provide a home for a wide variety of animals, and the aquatic grasses there filter out **pollutants**. But shoreline development has wrecked many tidal marshes. More than half have been eliminated in the United States.

A bioswale is a landscape element designed to keep pollutants from flowing into lakes, rivers, and tidal marshes. One type of bioswale is a planted area within or around a parking lot. The planted area takes the place of storm drains. How does it work? Rain falls or snow melts. The water runs off the pavement and into the soil. It will soak down into the soil until it reaches an aquifer. But first the soil and plant roots trap contaminants from the vehicles. These are things such as gas, oil, and pieces of metal or rubber. Over time, bacteria in the dirt break down many of these particles. They actually change the chemical structure so that these things are no longer toxic.

*This does not include Alaska.

People Affect Water

Directions: Darken the best answer choice.

1. Which is a bioswale designed to filter out?
   - Ⓐ a plastic bag
   - Ⓑ exhaust fumes
   - Ⓒ paper receipts
   - Ⓓ gasoline

2. The word **pollutants** means
   - Ⓐ harmful substances.
   - Ⓑ single-celled animals.
   - Ⓒ viruses.
   - Ⓓ helpful substances.

3. Which event occurred third?
   - Ⓐ People discovered an aquifer.
   - Ⓑ The water table fell.
   - Ⓒ People removed groundwater.
   - Ⓓ The land above the aquifer collapsed.

4. How does a swamp help to provide for the water demands of the population in a nearby city?
   - Ⓐ It makes water pure enough to drink without chemical treatment.
   - Ⓑ It treats sewage.
   - Ⓒ It provides a reservoir for creating electrical power.
   - Ⓓ It keeps the water table from getting too low.

5. Tidal marshes are in danger because people are
   - Ⓐ constructing cabins in forested areas.
   - Ⓑ putting up hotels and homes along the seashore.
   - Ⓒ building airports in coastal cities.
   - Ⓓ creating national parks along the coast.

6. The capital of the United States was built on reclaimed wetlands. This city is
   - Ⓐ Phoenix, Arizona.
   - Ⓑ Boston, Massachusetts.
   - Ⓒ Washington, D.C.
   - Ⓓ San Francisco, California.

A Natural Disaster: Hurricane Katrina

Hurricane Katrina was a big storm. It was one of the worst to ever strike the United States. Like all hurricanes, it formed over warm seawater. On August 25, 2005, it brushed the tip of Florida. It didn't cause too much harm. But then the storm moved across the Gulf of Mexico. It got stronger. It gathered speed. It picked up water. Then, it made landfall on August 29. It hit near the Louisiana-Mississippi border.

A storm surge comes before a hurricane. It reaches shore first. A storm surge has high waves. It causes a flood. Weather forecasters said that the storm was headed for New Orleans. This city is in Louisiana. It lies below sea level! Concrete walls are built around it. They are called levees. They are there to hold back storm surges. People were told to leave the city. But many old and poor people had no way to leave.

Hurricane Katrina's high winds and giant waves wiped out parts of three states. The states were Louisiana, Mississippi, and Alabama. In Biloxi and Gulfport, Mississippi, the storm surge was twenty-nine feet high. That is as tall as a four-story building! Much of both cities vanished. The rest of the buildings were ruined.

Four of the New Orleans levees broke. Water flooded 80 percent of the city. In some places, it was twenty-feet deep. It covered the roofs of one-story homes. And it was dirty water. It had sewage, gas, dead animals, mud, and debris in it.

For a week after the storm, dead bodies floated in the streets. Hundreds of people were stranded. Many were stuck on their roofs. Others were on highway overpasses. All of them had no food, water, or toilets. All of these people had to be saved by helicopters or boats. More than 20,000 people were inside a sports stadium. They ran out of food and water.

No one in the city had drinking water. No one had electric power. Things were really bad in hospitals and nursing homes, too. To keep very ill people alive, nurses worked **ventilators** by hand. They had to do this twenty-four hours a day. Otherwise the patients could not breathe.

Rescue teams worked day and night. It took a week to get everyone out of the city. They went to shelters in other states. A month passed before everyone had a roof over his or her head. About half a million people left. Many chose not to come back.

The storm killed more than 1,700 people. It left hundreds of thousands without homes. It took billions of dollars and many years to rebuild the area. This storm made the U.S. government see the need to improve emergency plans. It's important to be prepared before the next huge hurricane hits.

A Natural Disaster:
Hurricane Katrina

Hurricane Katrina was one of the worst storms ever to strike the United States. Like all hurricanes, it was a huge, swirling storm. It formed over warm seawater. On August 25, 2005, the storm brushed the tip of Florida. It didn't cause too much damage. But then the storm spun across the Gulf of Mexico. It grew stronger. It gathered speed and moisture. Then, it made landfall near the Louisiana-Mississippi border on August 29.

Before any hurricane reaches shore, a storm surge hits the coast. These high waves cause flooding. The day before the storm struck, weather forecasters said that it was headed for New Orleans. This city is in Louisiana. It lies below sea level! Concrete walls called levees are built around it. They are meant to hold back storm surges. As the storm bore down on them, people were told to leave the city. But many old and poor people had no way to leave.

Hurricane Katrina's high winds and giant waves wiped out parts of three states. The states were Louisiana, Mississippi, and Alabama. In Biloxi and Gulfport, Mississippi, the storm surge was twenty-nine feet high. That's as tall as a four-story building! Much of both of these cities vanished. The rest of the buildings were ruined.

New Orleans had the worst loss of life. Four of its levees broke. This let water flood 80 percent of the city. In some places, the water was twenty-feet deep. It covered the roofs of one-story homes. And it was dirty water. It had sewage, gas, dead animals, mud, and debris in it.

For a week after the storm, the news showed images of dead bodies floating in the streets. Hundreds of people were stuck on roofs. Hundreds more were stranded on highway overpasses. They had no food, water, or toilets. All of these people had to be rescued by helicopters or boats. More than 20,000 people were inside a sports stadium. They quickly ran out of food and water.

No one in the city had drinking water or electric power. The situation was bad in hospitals and nursing homes, too. To keep seriously ill people alive, nurses worked **ventilators** by hand. They had to do this twenty-four hours a day. Otherwise the patients could not breathe.

Rescue teams worked day and night. It took a week to get everyone out of the city. They went to shelters in other states. A month passed before everyone had a roof over his or her head. About half a million people left the city. Many chose not to return.

Hurricane Katrina killed more than 1,700 people. It left hundreds of thousands homeless. It took billions of dollars and many years to restore the area. This storm made the U.S. government see the need to improve emergency plans before the next huge hurricane.

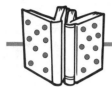

A Natural Disaster:
Hurricane Katrina

Hurricane Katrina was one of the worst storms ever to strike the United States. Like all hurricanes, it was a huge, swirling storm that formed over warm seawater. On August 25, 2005, the storm grazed the tip of Florida without causing much damage. But then the storm grew stronger. It gathered speed and moisture as it spun across the Gulf of Mexico. Then it made landfall near the Louisiana-Mississippi border on the morning of August 29.

Before any hurricane reaches shore, a storm surge hits the coast. These high waves cause flooding. The day before the storm struck, weather forecasters said that it was headed for New Orleans. The city is in Louisiana. It actually lies below sea level! Concrete walls called levees surround it. They were built to hold back storm surges. As the storm bore down on them, people were told to get out of the city. But many of the poor and elderly had no way to leave.

Hurricane Katrina's high winds and giant waves wiped out parts of Louisiana, Mississippi, and Alabama. In Biloxi and Gulfport, Mississippi, the storm surge was twenty-nine feet high. That's about the height of a four-story building! Much of both of these cities vanished, and the rest of the buildings were ruined.

New Orleans had the worst loss of life. Four of its levees broke. Water flooded 80 percent of the city. In some places, the water was twenty-feet deep. It covered the roofs of one-story homes. And it was dirty water. It had sewage, gas, dead animals, mud, and debris in it.

For a week after the storm, the news showed images of dead bodies floating in the streets. Hundreds of people were stuck on roofs. Hundreds more were stranded on highway overpasses with no food, water, or toilets. All of these people had to be rescued by helicopters or boats. More than 20,000 people were inside a sports stadium. They quickly ran out of food and water.

No one in the city had drinking water or electric power. The situation was bad in hospitals and nursing homes, too. To keep seriously ill people alive, nurses had to work **ventilators** by hand twenty-four hours a day. Otherwise the patents could not breathe.

Rescue teams worked day and night for a week to get everyone out of the city. They went to shelters in other states. Even so, a month passed before everyone had a roof over his or her head. About half a million people left the city. Many chose not to return.

Hurricane Katrina killed more than 1,700 people and left hundreds of thousands homeless. It took billions of dollars and many years to restore the area. This storm made the U.S. government see that it must improve emergency plans before the next big hurricane.

A Natural Disaster: Hurricane Katrina

Directions: Darken the best answer choice.

1. Hurricane Katrina did *not* cause major damage in the state of
   Ⓐ Mississippi.
   Ⓑ Florida.
   Ⓒ Alabama.
   Ⓓ Louisiana.

2. **Ventilators** are devices that
   Ⓐ direct emergency personnel to an injured person's location.
   Ⓑ stop fires from spreading.
   Ⓒ prevent heart attacks.
   Ⓓ help people to inhale and exhale.

3. Which event occurred third?
   Ⓐ Hurricane Katrina spun across the Atlantic Ocean.
   Ⓑ Hurricane Katrina's storm surge struck shore.
   Ⓒ Hurricane Katrina spun across the Gulf of Mexico.
   Ⓓ Levees broke and flooded New Orleans.

4. Why did so many people have to be rescued by helicopter?
   Ⓐ Only helicopters could withstand the storm surge.
   Ⓑ No other rescue vehicles were available.
   Ⓒ People had gone to the highest places to keep from drowning.
   Ⓓ Police and city rescue workers were on strike.

5. What is unusual about the city of New Orleans?
   Ⓐ It is built below sea level.
   Ⓑ It is often destroyed by huge hurricanes.
   Ⓒ Frequent storms knock out its electrical power grid.
   Ⓓ Most of the people who live there have no way to leave the city.

6. Why was it dangerous for people to be without clean water after the storm?
   Ⓐ They might drink dirty water and die.
   Ⓑ They could not take a shower.
   Ⓒ They could die of starvation.
   Ⓓ They might drown in filthy water.

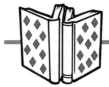

Is That the Wind? No, It's Energy!

Wind power is **kinetic** energy. It comes from air blowing over Earth's surface. Kinetic energy comes from movement. Wind is a renewable energy. That means that it can't get used up. Winds will always blow. They are part of our weather. If we could catch just one-tenth of Earth's winds each year, we would have more energy than what the whole world uses in a year! Wind is clean energy, too. Using it does not pollute air, water, or soil.

People have used wind power for thousands of years. Long ago, someone thought of making a sail to move a boat. Over time, bigger and bigger ships were moved by wind-filling sails. Windmills have been used for thousands of years, too. They may have been first built in what is now Iran. Windmills have blades. The blades turn when the wind hits them. The turning blades spin a shaft. Early windmills used the spinning shaft to turn millstones. Wheat was laid between these millstones. It was ground into flour.

In the Netherlands, windmills have been in use for a long time. They pump water off land. This keeps the land dry. Why? The people had reclaimed the land from the sea. The sea is always trying to re-cover the land with water. In early America, windmills were built to drive pumps. They lifted water from below ground. The water filled troughs. Then, farm animals drank from them.

Now, we build wind turbines to make electric power. Today, there are more than 25,000 wind turbines around the world. But we don't have these machines perfected. Right now, wind turbines change less than half of the wind hitting their blades into energy. Engineers are working on this. They want to make the turbines work better.

Scientists must think about many things before building a wind farm. Wind speeds vary from place to place. Some sites are worse than others. In general, an open hilltop that's not blocked by trees is best. Many such hilltops are farm fields. The turbines can stand on farmland that is being farmed. The farmer can drive a tractor around them. This lets the land be used for two purposes at the same time. Some wind turbines have been built offshore. They catch the ocean breezes. No matter where the turbines are built, some people do not like how they look. They do not want to live near them.

Wind does not blow at a constant speed. It does not blow all of the time. Yet people need a supply of electric power that they can depend on. Wind turbines cannot provide all our electricity. They must have a backup generator that uses another energy source.

Is That the Wind? No, It's Energy!

Wind power is **kinetic** energy. It comes from air blowing over Earth's surface. Kinetic energy comes from movement. Wind is a renewable energy since it can't get used up. Winds will always blow. They are part of our weather. If we could catch just one-tenth of Earth's winds each year, we would have more energy than what the whole world uses in a year! Wind is clean energy, too, because it does not pollute air, water, or soil.

People have used wind power for thousands of years. Long ago, someone thought of making a sail to move a boat. Over time, bigger and bigger ships were moved by wind-filling, large sails. Windmills have been used for thousands of years, too. They were probably first built in what is now Iran. Windmills have blades that turn when the wind hits them. The turning blades spin a shaft. Early windmills used the spinning shaft to move millstones. Wheat was laid between these millstones and then ground into flour.

In the Netherlands, windmills have been in use for a long time. They pump water off the land to keep it dry. Why? The people reclaimed the land from the sea. The sea is always trying to re-cover the land with water. In early America, windmills operated pumps. The pumps lifted water from below ground. The water filled troughs. Then, farm animals drank from them.

Now, we build wind turbines to make electric power. Today, more than 25,000 wind turbines operate around the world. But we don't have these machines perfected. Right now, wind turbines only change less than half of the wind hitting their blades into energy. Engineers are working on making the turbines more efficient.

Scientists must think about a lot of factors before building a wind farm. Wind speeds vary from place to place. Some sites are worse than others. In general, an open hilltop not blocked by trees is best. Many such hilltops are farm fields. But that's okay. Turbines can stand on land that is being farmed. The farmer can drive a tractor around them. This lets the land be used for two purposes at once. Wind turbines have been built offshore to catch the ocean breezes, too. Even when a great site is found, some people may protest. They dislike how wind turbines look and do not want to live near them.

Wind does not blow at a constant speed, and it does not blow all of the time. Yet people need a supply of electric power that they can depend on. Wind turbines will never provide all our electricity. They must have a backup generator with a different energy source.

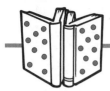

Is That the Wind? No, It's Energy!

Wind power is **kinetic** energy that comes from air blowing over Earth's surface. Kinetic energy comes from movement. Wind is a renewable energy. That means that it can't get used up. Why? Winds will always blow. They are part of our atmosphere and weather. If we could collect just one-tenth of Earth's winds each year, we would have more energy than the annual energy needs of the whole world! Also, wind is clean energy. Using it does not pollute air, water, or soil.

People have been using wind power for thousands of years, especially to move ships. Windmills have been used for thousands of years, too. They probably were first invented in what is now Iran. Windmills have blades that turn when the wind hits them. The turning blades make a shaft spin. Early windmills used the spinning to turn millstones that would grind wheat into flour.

In the Netherlands, windmills have long been used to pump water to keep the land that the people had reclaimed from the sea dry. In early America, windmills were built to operate pumps and lift water from below ground to troughs from which farm animals would drink.

Today, we build wind turbines to generate, or make, electric power. More than 25,000 of these wind turbines are operating worldwide. But we don't have these machines perfected yet. Right now, wind turbines change less than half of the wind striking their blades into rotational energy. Engineers are working to improve the turbines' efficiency.

Scientists have to consider many factors before building a wind farm. Wind speeds vary from place to place. Some sites are much better than others. In general, an open hilltop that's not blocked by trees is ideal. Many such hilltops are farmland. Fortunately, the land can be used for two purposes at the same time. The turbines stand on farmland, and the farmer can just drive a tractor around them. Wind turbines have even been built offshore in order to capture ocean breezes. Some people dislike how wind turbines look. They don't want to live near them. This means that even once a good site is found, some people protest against the building of a wind farm.

Unfortunately, wind does not blow at a constant speed, or even all of the time. Yet people need a constant supply of electricity that's always available. Wind turbines must be combined with a backup generator that uses a different energy source.

Is That the Wind? No, It's Energy!

Directions: Darken the best answer choice.

1. One problem with relying on electricity made by wind power is that
   - Ⓐ wind power is not renewable.
   - Ⓑ the wind does not blow all the time.
   - Ⓒ the turbines take up valuable farmland.
   - Ⓓ wind power causes air pollution.

2. The word **kinetic** means
   - Ⓐ nonpolluting.
   - Ⓑ expensive.
   - Ⓒ movement.
   - Ⓓ inexpensive.

3. Which is the most recent use of wind power?
   - Ⓐ to move ships
   - Ⓑ to grind grain such as corn or wheat
   - Ⓒ to provide water for animals
   - Ⓓ to make electricity

4. Archaeologists think that windmills were invented in
   - Ⓐ Europe.
   - Ⓑ the Middle East.
   - Ⓒ North America.
   - Ⓓ Africa.

5. A future goal that wind engineers are working toward is to find a way to
   - Ⓐ stop air pollution.
   - Ⓑ let farmers use the land on which wind turbines stand.
   - Ⓒ make the wind blow more consistently.
   - Ⓓ store the energy generated by wind turbines.

6. You can tell that a *trough* is a
   - Ⓐ container for water.
   - Ⓑ type of wind turbine.
   - Ⓒ kind of ship's sail.
   - Ⓓ pump used by farmers.

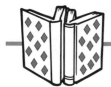

Jane Addams, Social Reformer

Jane Addams was the first American woman to win the Nobel Peace Prize. This prize has been given each year since 1898. It is for the person who has done the most to encourage peace. The winner gets a medal. He or she gets a big cash prize, too. Jane did not keep the money for herself. She used it to help others.

In 1860, Jane was born into a rich family in Illinois. Having money did not shield her from sadness. Her mother died when she was four. Her sister died when she was eight. Jane suffered from a damaged spine. She had back pain for most of her life.

Jane loved to read. At a young age, she knew she would get a college degree. This was at a time when almost no women went to college. After she finished her degree, she decided to become a doctor. At that time, it was not a job for a woman. Jane was determined. Yet it was not to be. She fell ill. She grew so weak that she gave up her plans to be a doctor.

To recover, Jane took a trip abroad. There, she saw a settlement house. It was in a poor part of town. College students from Oxford and Cambridge lived in this house. They were there to help the needy people of London. Jane got excited. She and her friend, Ellen Starr, bought a big, old house in Chicago. They fixed it up. They opened their own settlement house. They named it Hull House. The two founders lived there. Other young women who did not have to work for a living came to help them. The volunteers held free classes to teach adults to read. They helped immigrants learn to speak English. There was baby care for working parents. Sick people got care. Within two years of opening, 2,000 people were getting help from Hull House each week!

Jane never had any children. But she loved kids. At that time, child labor was a fact of life. Kids as young as six worked all day. They ran dangerous machines in factories. They had no time for school. Jane fought against this. She felt that children should not work. She wanted them to learn and play. So in 1893, she opened the first public playground. Jane also worked to get women the right to vote.

People gave cash to help Hull House. By 1907, it had grown to twelve buildings. In 1910, Jane received the first honorary degree Yale University ever awarded to a woman. The public loved her. Then, America entered World War I in 1917. Some people turned against Jane. She was a **pacifist**. She spoke out against the war. Many people felt that patriotism meant supporting the nation's decision to join the war. A lot of people thought that pacifists did not honor the brave troops in battle. When Jane sent supplies to the women and children in the enemy nations, the newspapers wrote pieces against her.

Jane Addams

After the U.S. won the war, Jane's popularity returned. People were glad when she won the Nobel Peace Prize in 1931. Jane died four years later. At her funeral, people honored her as one of the most influential social reformers in the world.

Jane Addams, Social Reformer

Jane Addams was the first American woman to win the Nobel Peace Prize. Since 1898, this prize has been given out each year to the person who has done the most to encourage peace. The winner receives a medal. He or she gets a large cash prize as well. Jane did not keep the money for herself. She used it to help others.

In 1860, Jane was born into a rich family in Illinois, but having money did not shield her from sadness. Her mother died when she was four. Her sister died when she was eight. Jane suffered from a damaged spine and had back pain for most of her life.

Jane loved to read. At a young age, she knew she wanted to earn a college degree. This was at a time when almost no women went to college. When she finished her degree, she decided to go on to become a doctor. At that time, it was not a job for a woman, but Jane was determined. Yet it was not to be. She fell ill. She grew so weak that she gave up her plans to go to medical school.

To recover, Jane took a trip abroad. There, she saw a settlement house. It was in a poor part of town. College students from Oxford and Cambridge lived in this house. They were there to help the poorest people of London. Jane got excited. She and her friend, Ellen Starr, bought a big, old house in Chicago. They fixed it up and opened their own settlement house. They named it Hull House. The two founders lived there. Other young women who did not have to work for a living came to help them. The volunteers taught free classes, so adults could learn to read. They helped immigrants to learn to speak English. There was baby care for working parents. Sick people were nursed. Within two years of opening, 2,000 people were receiving help from Hull House every week!

Jane never had any children, but she loved kids. At that time, child labor was common. Kids as young as six worked all day in factories. They ran dangerous machines. Jane fought against this. She felt that children should go to school and have time to play. So in 1893, she opened the first public playground. Jane also worked to get women the right to vote.

People supported Hull House with cash donations. By 1907, it had grown to twelve buildings. In 1910, Jane received the first honorary degree Yale University ever awarded to a woman. The public loved her. Then, America entered World War I in 1917, and some people turned against Jane. She was a **pacifist** and spoke out against the war. Many people felt that it was not patriotic to disagree with the nation's decision to join the war. A lot of people thought that pacifists dishonored the troops engaged in battle. When Jane sent supplies to the women and children in the enemy nations, several newspapers wrote pieces attacking her.

Jane Addams

After the U.S. won the war, Jane's popularity returned. People were pleased when she won the Nobel Peace Prize in 1931. When Jane died four years later, people honored her as one of the most influential social reformers in the world.

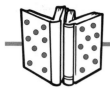

Jane Addams, Social Reformer

Jane Addams was the first American woman to win the Nobel Peace Prize. Since 1898, this prize has been given out each year to the person who has done the most to promote or maintain peace. The winner receives a medal and a large cash prize. Jane did not keep this money for herself. She used it to help others.

In 1860, Jane was born into a wealthy family in Illinois, but having money did not shield her from tragedy. Her mother died when she was four, and her sister died when she was eight. Jane had a damaged spine, and she suffered from back pain for most of her life.

Jane loved to read and, at an early age, decided she would get a college education at a time when almost no women went to college. After she completed her degree, she decided to continue on and become a doctor. At that time, it was an unheard-of profession for a woman. Jane was determined, but it was not to be. She fell ill. She was so weak that she gave up her plans to go to medical school.

To recover, Jane took a trip abroad. There, she first saw a settlement house. College students from Oxford and Cambridge lived in this settlement house in a poor part of town. They provided help to the impoverished people of London. Jane got excited. She and her friend, Ellen Starr, bought an old mansion in Chicago. They fixed it up and opened their own settlement house named Hull House. The two founders lived there. More young women who did not have to work for a living joined them. The volunteers held free classes to teach adults to read and immigrants to speak English. They offered baby care for working parents. Sick people received nursing care. Within two years of opening, 2,000 people were receiving help from Hull House every week!

Jane never had any children, but she loved kids. At that time, child labor was a fact of life. Kids as young as six ran dangerous machines in factories. Jane fought against this practice. She felt that kids should not work. She wanted them to spend time in school and playing. So in 1893, she opened the first public playground. Jane also worked tirelessly to get women the right to vote.

People supported Hull House with donations, and by 1907, it had grown to twelve buildings. In 1910, she received the first honorary degree Yale University had ever awarded to a woman. Jane was very popular with the public. However, after America entered World War I in 1917, some turned against her. Jane was an outspoken **pacifist**. She was against fighting in the war. Many people felt that patriotism meant supporting the nation's decision to join the war and that pacifists dishonored the troops engaged in battle. When Jane provided supplies to help the women and children in the enemy nations, several newspapers wrote pieces attacking her.

Jane Addams

After the U.S. won the war, Jane's popularity returned. People were pleased when she won the Nobel Peace Prize in 1931. When she died four years later, the public honored her as one of the most influential social reformers in the world.

Jane Addams, Social Reformer

Directions: Darken the best answer choice.

1. Jane Addams led a life of "firsts." Which one of these was *not* one of them?
   - Ⓐ opening the world's first settlement house
   - Ⓑ opening the first public playground for children
   - Ⓒ being the first woman to earn an honorary degree from Yale University
   - Ⓓ opening the first settlement house in America

2. A **pacifist** is a person who
   - Ⓐ helps the enemy during a war.
   - Ⓑ works as a spy for the enemy.
   - Ⓒ works as a spy for one's own nation.
   - Ⓓ is against the use of violence in any situation.

3. Which of these events occurred second?
   - Ⓐ Jane started Hull House.
   - Ⓑ Jane earned a college degree.
   - Ⓒ Jane traveled to London.
   - Ⓓ Jane won the Nobel Peace Prize.

4. During one point in her life, many people turned against Jane. Why?
   - Ⓐ She earned a college degree, which at that time was considered shocking for a woman.
   - Ⓑ She spoke out against America's involvement in World War I.
   - Ⓒ She was active in the movement to get women the right to vote.
   - Ⓓ She was against child labor.

5. What prompted Jane to open Hull House?
   - Ⓐ She wanted to run a settlement house like the one she'd visited in England.
   - Ⓑ Her mother and sister had died because they did not receive medical care.
   - Ⓒ She wanted to win a Nobel Peace Prize.
   - Ⓓ She hoped to earn an honorary degree from Yale University.

6. Jane died when she was about
   - Ⓐ fifty-five years old.
   - Ⓑ sixty-five years old.
   - Ⓒ seventy-five years old.
   - Ⓓ eighty-five years old.

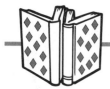

Different Viewpoints in History

Sometimes two groups will not see things the same way. It causes big problems between them. The Native Americans were living here when the European settlers arrived. The Native Americans did not believe that a person could own land. They thought that people could live on land but never claim it as their own. The Europeans thought that owning land was very important. In Europe, those who owned land were rich. They were in charge. The white settlers felt as excited about owning land as you would feel if someone gave you a million dollars. The settlers "bought" land from the Native Americans. They paid with glass beads and other not-too-valuable things. But the Native Americans didn't understand the concept of selling land. Remember, they didn't think it could be bought, sold, or traded. They thought the newcomers would just share the land. They didn't understand fences. They didn't know about borders. This difference in viewpoint caused a lot of fighting between the two groups.

Slavery was once part of the American culture. It's hard to believe, but many years ago, people saw it as acceptable. It was how things had always been done. Even great men in our history, like Thomas Jefferson, had slaves. He even said it was wrong. He did not beat them. He did not mistreat them. But he didn't set them free until he died. **Abolitionists** wanted to end slavery. They had to convince Americans that one human being should not own another. It took a lot of time and effort. At last, the people in the North agreed. But those in the South did not. That's why the U.S. Civil War was fought. The South wanted things to go on as they always had. The plantations in the South had many slaves. The plantation owners said their farms had to have free labor. Without it, they would not survive.

The Southern states withdrew from the Union. They said they were a new nation. Then, they could have slaves. U.S. President Abraham Lincoln said no. He said they could not leave the Union. The fight began. It lasted five long, bloody years. When it ended, the nation reunited. The slaves were set free. But it took a long time to change how some Southerners viewed African Americans.

One hundred years ago, American women could not vote. They could not control money. They could not inherit property. They could not own businesses. Back then, many people said that women were weak. Men had to take care of them. They couldn't take care of themselves. Both men and women had been raised to think this way. Even many women thought it was true. Luckily, some women knew better. They were suffragists. They gave speeches. They wrote booklets. They argued that women had the right to vote. In 1920, women did get voting rights. How did that change things? Women got a say in government. This let them influence the laws. At last, women could have their own money. They could buy houses. They could start businesses. Even so, it took a long time for them to be treated as men's equals.

Different Viewpoints in History

Sometimes two groups will see things differently. It causes big problems between them. The Native Americans who were living here when the European settlers arrived did not believe that a person could own land. They thought that people could live on land but never claim it as their own. The Europeans thought that owning land was very important. In Europe, those who owned land were wealthy. They were in control. The white settlers felt as excited about owning land as you would feel if someone gave you a million dollars. The settlers "bought" land from the Native Americans. They paid with glass beads and other not-too-valuable items. But the Native Americans didn't understand the concept of selling land. Remember, they didn't think it could be bought, sold, or traded. They thought the newcomers would just share the land. They didn't understand fences and borders. This difference in viewpoint caused a lot of bloodshed between the two groups.

Slavery was once part of the American culture. It's hard to believe, but people once saw it as acceptable. It was how things had always been done. Even great men in our history, like Thomas Jefferson, who said that slavery was wrong, owned slaves. He did not beat them or mistreat them. Still, he didn't set them free until he died. It took **abolitionists** a lot of time and effort to convince Americans that one human being should not own another. And even once the people in the North agreed, those in the South did not. That's why the U.S. Civil War was fought. The South wanted things to go on as they always had. The plantations in the South had many slaves. The plantation owners said their farms could not survive without free labor.

The Southern states withdrew from the Union. They said they were a new nation. Then, they could have slaves. U.S. President Abraham Lincoln said they could not leave the Union. The fight began. After five long, bloody years, it ended. The nation was reunited. The slaves were set free. But it took a long time to change how some Southerners viewed African Americans.

One hundred years ago, American women could not vote. They could not control money, inherit property, or own businesses. At that time, many people said that women were weak. Men had to take care of them. They couldn't possibly take care of themselves. Both men and women had been raised to think this way. Even many women thought they were not as capable as men. Fortunately, there were some women who knew better. They were suffragists. They gave speeches and wrote booklets. They argued that women must be given the right to vote. In 1920, women did get voting rights. How did that change things? Once women had a say in government, they could influence the laws. At last, women could have their own money, buy houses, hold jobs, or start businesses. Even so, it took a long time for them to be treated as men's equals.

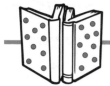

Different Viewpoints in History

Sometimes when two groups see things differently, it causes big problems between them. The Native Americans who were living here when the European settlers arrived did not believe that a person could own land. They thought that people could live on land but never claim it as their own. The Europeans thought that owning land was very important. In Europe, those who owned land were wealthy and in control. The white settlers felt as excited about owning land as you would feel if someone gave you a million dollars. The settlers "bought" land from the Native Americans. They paid with glass beads and other not-too-valuable items. But the Native Americans didn't understand the concept of selling land. Remember, they didn't think it could be bought, sold, or traded. They thought the newcomers would just share the land. They didn't understand fences and borders. This difference in viewpoint caused a lot of bloodshed between the two groups.

Slavery was once part of the American culture. It seems hard to believe, but people saw it as acceptable. It was how things had always been done. Even great men in our history, like Thomas Jefferson, who said that slavery was wrong, owned slaves. Although he did not beat them or mistreat them, he didn't set them free until he died. It took **abolitionists** a lot of time and effort to convince Americans that one human being should not own another. Even once the people in the North agreed, those in the South did not. That's why the U.S. Civil War was fought. The South wanted things to continue as they always had. The plantations in the South had many slaves, and the owners said the plantations could not survive without free labor.

The Southern states withdrew from the Union and claimed they were a new nation. Then, they could have slaves. U.S. President Abraham Lincoln said they could not leave the Union. The war lasted five long, bloody years. When the war was over, the nation was reunited, and the slaves were set free. But it took a long time to change how some Southerners viewed African Americans.

One hundred years ago, American women could not vote. They could not control money, inherit property, or own businesses. In those days, many people thought that women were weak and men had to take care of them because they couldn't possibly take care of themselves. Both men and women had been raised to think this way. Many women even thought they were not as capable as men. Fortunately, some women knew better. These suffragists gave speeches and wrote pamphlets. They argued that women should have the right to vote. In 1920, women did get voting rights. Once women had a say in government, they influenced the laws. At last, women could have their own money, buy houses, hold jobs, or start businesses. Even so, it took a long time before they were treated as men's equals.

Different Viewpoints in History

Directions: Darken the best answer choice.

1. During the Civil War, the Northern states fought to make sure that
   - Ⓐ women could vote.
   - Ⓑ women could not vote.
   - Ⓒ slavery would end.
   - Ⓓ slavery would continue.

2. An **abolitionist** is a person who is
   - Ⓐ for women's rights.
   - Ⓑ against slavery.
   - Ⓒ a Civil War soldier.
   - Ⓓ trying to restore land to Native American tribes.

3. Which of these events happened first?
   - Ⓐ European settlers took over Native American lands.
   - Ⓑ Women earned the right to vote.
   - Ⓒ The U.S. Civil War was fought.
   - Ⓓ Abolitionists protested.

4. Which statement is true?
   - Ⓐ The Southern states withdrew from the Union so that their women could vote.
   - Ⓑ Abolitionists promoted slavery on Southern plantations.
   - Ⓒ Native Americans did not understand the idea of land ownership.
   - Ⓓ Native Americans caused the U.S. Civil War.

5. Which is an example of a person saying one thing while doing the opposite?
   - Ⓐ a suffragist demanding the right to vote in an election
   - Ⓑ Abraham Lincoln refusing to let states leave the Union
   - Ⓒ a European leader paying for land with beads and other trinkets
   - Ⓓ Thomas Jefferson owning slaves

6. Which group "fought" using methods that were most like the suffragists' methods?
   - Ⓐ Native Americans
   - Ⓑ abolitionists
   - Ⓒ Civil War soldiers
   - Ⓓ European settlers

Colin Powell,
Former U.S. Secretary of State

Colin Powell was born in 1937. He lived in New York City. His parents told him to do his best. They said, "Whatever you do, do with excellence." Colin did just that.

When Colin was seventeen, he went to college. He joined the army, too. How did he do both? He joined Reserve Officers' Training Corps (ROTC). He took academic and military classes at the same time. He worked hard. He was one of the best students to ever go through the ROTC program.

Colin got married. He had children. Then, he fought in the Vietnam War. He was brave and earned awards. He earned the Purple Heart. He earned one Bronze Star. He became a general. Then, he went back to college. He got a new degree. Next, Colin led troops in Korea. The troops were doing things wrong. He made them behave.

By now, people had noticed Colin. They saw that he did any task well. He went to Washington, D.C. He worked in the Defense Department. He served as National Security Advisor. He worked for President Ronald Reagan. This was in the 1980s.

In August 1990, there was trouble in the Middle East. The nation of Iraq invaded a nearby land. It took over tiny Kuwait. U.S. President George H. W. Bush told the Iraqis to go home. They stayed. So in January 1991, the U.S. sent troops. The soldiers did great. They won the war. It took them just forty-three days. How? President Bush had relied on Colin. At that time, he was the chairman of the Joint Chiefs of Staff. This means he was the top-ranking U.S. military officer. He was the first African American to hold this post. He was also the youngest chairman ever. The Persian Gulf War made Colin a hero. Two years later, he retired. He wrote a book about his life.

People told Colin to try for the presidency. But he did not want to run. Instead, George W. Bush, the son of the former president, became president. When he took office, he asked Colin to fill a key position. Colin became the U.S. Secretary of State. He was the first African American to do so. In this role, he talked to the president about world affairs. He acted for the president in meetings. He met with leaders around the globe.

Colin Powell

On September 11, 2001, terrorists attacked America. Colin helped decide what to do. He told Bush to remove the leaders from the nation of Afghanistan. Colin got other nations to help. They joined the U.S. troops in the fight.

Colin is an American hero. He served the U.S. for a long time. He did each of his jobs well. What is his advice to you? "There is no **substitute** for hard work and study. Nothing comes easy. You must be ready for opportunity when it comes."

Colin Powell, Former U.S. Secretary of State

Colin Powell was born in New York City in 1937. His parents told him to always do his best. They said, "Whatever you do, do with excellence." Colin took those words to heart. He followed them all his life.

Colin went to college and joined the military. He was just seventeen years old. How did he do both at the same time? He joined Reserve Officers' Training Corps (ROTC). This means that he took both academic and military classes. He worked hard and made a name for himself. He was one of the best recruits to ever go through the ROTC program.

Colin got married and had children. Then, he fought in the Vietnam War. There, he earned the Purple Heart. He earned one Bronze Star, too. He was also promoted to general. When he came home, he went back to college. He got a master's degree. Next, he led an infantry division in Korea. The troops were doing things wrong, but he made them straighten up.

By now, people had noticed Colin. They saw that he did well at any task he took on. They knew he would do great things. He went to Washington, D.C. and worked in the Defense Department. Then, he served as a National Security Advisor to President Ronald Reagan. This was in the 1980s.

In August 1990, the nation of Iraq attacked the nearby nation of Kuwait. Both are in the Middle East. U.S. President George H. W. Bush told the Iraqis to leave. Their leader refused. So, in January 1991, the U.S. sent soldiers to remove the invaders. The troops did so well that they won the war in just forty-three days. To do this, President Bush had relied on Colin. At that time, he was the chairman of the Joint Chiefs of Staff. In this job, he was the highest-ranking U.S. military officer. He was the first African American to hold this important post. He was also the youngest chairman ever. The Persian Gulf War made Powell a hero. In 1993, Colin retired. He wrote a book about his life. Its title is *My American Journey.*

Many people felt that Colin should run for the presidency. However, Colin did not want to run for office. President George W. Bush was the son of the former president. When he took office, he asked Colin to take a key position. Colin became the U.S. Secretary of State. He was the first African American to do so. In this role, he advised the president on foreign affairs. He represented the president in meetings with other leaders from around the world.

Colin Powell

On September 11, 2001, terrorists attacked America. He helped the president decide what to do. Colin said to remove the leaders from the nation of Afghanistan. Then, he got other nations to agree to help. They joined the U.S. troops.

Colin is an American hero who served the U.S. for a long time. He did each of his jobs well. What is his advice to you? "There is no **substitute** for hard work and study. Nothing comes easy. You must be ready for opportunity when it comes."

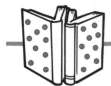

Colin Powell,
Former U.S. Secretary of State

Colin Powell was born in New York City in 1937. His parents told him, "Whatever you do, do with excellence." Colin took those words to heart and followed them all his life.

Colin went to college and joined the military when he was just seventeen years old. How did he do both at the same time? He joined Reserve Officers' Training Corps (ROTC). This means that he took both academic and military classes. He worked hard and made a name for himself. He was one of the best recruits to ever go through the ROTC program.

Colin got married and had children. Then, he fought in the Vietnam War. There, he earned some awards. He earned the Purple Heart, one Bronze Star, and was promoted to general. When he came home, he went back to college and earned a master's degree. Next, he led an infantry division in Korea. The troops were doing things wrong, but he quickly got them in good shape.

By now, people had noticed Colin. They saw that he did well at any task he took on and knew that he would do great things. He went to Washington, D.C. and worked in the Defense Department. Then, he served as National Security Advisor to President Ronald Reagan in the 1980s.

In August 1990, the nation of Iraq invaded the nearby nation of Kuwait. Both are in the Middle East. U.S. President George H. W. Bush told the Iraqis to leave. Their leader refused. So, in January 1991, the U.S. sent troops to remove the invaders. The soldiers performed so well that they won the war in just forty-three days. To do this, President Bush had relied on Colin. At that time, he was the chairman of the Joint Chiefs of Staff. In this job, he was the highest-ranking U.S. military officer. He was the first African American to hold this important post. He was also the youngest chairman ever. The Persian Gulf War made Powell a hero. In 1993, Colin retired and wrote a book about his life entitled *My American Journey.*

Many people suggested that Colin run for the presidency. However, Colin did not want to run for office. President George W. Bush, the son of the former president, became president. When he took office, he asked Colin to become the U.S. Secretary of State. He was the first African American to do so. In this role, he advised the president on foreign affairs. He represented the president in meetings with other leaders from around the world.

Colin Powell

On September 11, 2001, when terrorists attacked America, Colin helped the president decide what to do. He said to remove the leaders from the nation of Afghanistan. Then, he got other nations to agree to help by joining the U.S. troops.

Colin is an American hero who served the U.S. for a long time and did each of his jobs well. What is his advice to you? "There is no **substitute** for hard work and study. Nothing comes easy. You must be ready for opportunity when it comes."

Colin Powell, Former U.S. Secretary of State

Directions: Darken the best answer choice.

1. Colin Powell served as the U.S. Secretary of State under President
   Ⓐ George W. Bush.
   Ⓑ Bill Clinton.
   Ⓒ George H. W. Bush.
   Ⓓ Ronald Reagan.

2. The word **substitute** means
   Ⓐ assistance.
   Ⓑ encouragement.
   Ⓒ competition.
   Ⓓ replacement.

3. Which event happened second in Colin's life?
   Ⓐ Colin was the chairman of the Joint Chiefs of Staff.
   Ⓑ Colin fought in the Vietnam War.
   Ⓒ Colin joined ROTC.
   Ⓓ Colin became a general.

4. *My American Journey* is an example of a(n)
   Ⓐ Web site.
   Ⓑ work of fiction.
   Ⓒ autobiography.
   Ⓓ bibliography.

5. The United States' goal during the 1991 Persian Gulf War was to
   Ⓐ make the Iraqis withdraw from Kuwait.
   Ⓑ take control of Iraq.
   Ⓒ remove the leaders from Afghanistan.
   Ⓓ make the Kuwaitis withdraw from Iraq.

6. You can tell that Colin believed in
   Ⓐ starting wars in the Middle East.
   Ⓑ the importance of education.
   Ⓒ his ability to become U.S. president.
   Ⓓ trying to become famous.

Helping the Blind and Deaf Communicate

Louis Braille was born in 1809. He was able to see. But he had an accident when he was three years old. He was playing with a tool. He hit himself in the eye. Then, he got an **infection**. It spread to his good eye. He lost the sight in that eye, too. When he was ten, he went to the world's first school for the blind. He learned to read books. They had raised letters. But the method used to make the books cost a lot. It took a lot of labor, too. That's why the school had just fourteen books. Louis wanted to find a better way. When he was just fifteen, he invented Braille writing. He spent the rest of his life teaching people who were blind.

Braille is a writing system. It has raised dots inside cells. A blind person runs his or her finger across the dots. He or she recognizes the pattern. He or she knows each letter by using a fingertip. There are between two and six dots in each cell. Each cell stands for a letter, a numeral, or a punctuation mark. Often-used words and letter pairs (such as *th*) have their own single-cell patterns.

There are two grades of Braille. In Grade One, a person learns the twenty-six letters of the alphabet and punctuation. Beginners use Grade One. It is how they get started with Braille. In Grade Two, a person knows everything in Grade One plus learns contractions. The contractions are important. They save space. A Braille page cannot hold as much text as a printed page. Books, menus, public signs, and most Braille materials use Grade Two. Braille is used in many different languages,

including Chinese. Now, many books are on CD. Blind people can listen to them. But Braille is still the way that most blind people read and write.

Thomas Gallaudet was born in 1787. He was always smaller and weaker than other kids. He was often left out of their games, and he often felt rejected. He was smart. He graduated from Yale University at the age of seventeen. Thomas wanted all people to be included. He did not want anyone to be lonely. He saw that people often ignored deaf people. They could not follow a conversation. They were left out.

Thomas decided to do something about it. He started the first church and first free school for the deaf in the United States. Someone had already created a manual alphabet. It let people spell out words using their fingers. This manual alphabet is still used. Why? Sometimes a name or word must be spelled. But Thomas created American Sign Language. It is even better than the manual alphabet. Sign language has made things easier. One hand signal stands for a whole word. When a speaker is talking, an interpreter can keep up. The interpreter can hear. He or she knows sign language and the manual alphabet. He or she can use both to display a spoken message to a deaf person.

Today, deaf people can use the phone with their computer. First, they call a toll-free number. Then, they dial the person to whom they want to talk. A hearing person is the third party in the call. This person types the words that are spoken. These words show up on the computer screen. It's like the captions you may have seen on DVDs. The deaf person can see the words. And if he or she has some hearing, that person can get input from the phone. Some people have been able to use the phone for the first time with this system.

Helping the Blind and Deaf Communicate

Louis Braille was born in 1809 able to see. But he had an accident when he was three years old. He was playing with a tool and stabbed himself in the eye. To make matters worse, he got an **infection** that spread to his good eye. He lost the vision in that eye, too. When he was ten, he went to the world's first school for the blind. He learned to read books with raised letters. But the method used to make the books was expensive and took a lot of labor. The school had only fourteen books. Louis knew there had to be a better way. When he was just fifteen, he invented Braille writing. He spent the rest of his life teaching people who were blind.

Braille is a writing system made up of patterns of raised dots inside cells. A blind person can run his or her finger across the dots and recognize the pattern. He or she can tell what each letter is by using a fingertip. There can be between two and six dots in one cell. Each cell represents a letter, a numeral, or a punctuation mark. Some frequently used words and letter combinations (such as *th*) have their own single-cell patterns.

There are two grades of Braille. In Grade One, a person learns the twenty-six letters of the alphabet and punctuation. Beginners use Grade One to get started in Braille. In Grade Two, a person knows everything in Grade One plus learns contractions. The contractions are important. They save space since a Braille page cannot hold as much text as a printed page. All books, menus, public signs, and most Braille materials use Grade Two. Braille is used to write many different languages, including Chinese. Many books are now on CD, allowing blind people to listen to them. However, Braille is still the way that most blind people read and write.

Thomas Gallaudet was born in 1787. He was always smaller and weaker than other kids. He was often left out of their games and felt rejected. He was so smart that he graduated from Yale University at the age of seventeen. Thomas believed that all people should be included. No one should feel lonely. He noticed that people often ignored deaf people. They were left out. Why? They could not follow a conversation.

Thomas decided to do something about it. He started the first church and first free school for the deaf in the United States. Someone had already created a manual alphabet. With it, people spelled out words with their fingers. This manual alphabet is still used. Some names and words must be spelled. Thomas created American Sign Language. It made things easier. One hand signal means a whole word. This means that when a speaker is talking, an interpreter can keep up with the speaker. The interpreter can hear. He or she knows sign language and the manual alphabet. He or she can use both to relay the message to a deaf person.

Today, deaf people can use the phone with their computer. First, they call a toll-free number. Then, they dial the person to whom they want to talk. A hearing person is the third party in the call. This person types all the words that are spoken. These words appear on the computer screen. It's like the captions you may have seen on DVDs. The deaf person can see the words, and if he or she has any hearing, gets some input from the phone. Some people have been able to use the phone for the first time with this system.

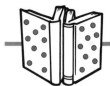

Helping the Blind
and Deaf Communicate

When Louis Braille was born in 1809, he was able to see. But he had a terrible accident when he was three years old. He was playing with a tool and stabbed himself in the eye. Then, he got an **infection** that spread to his good eye, and he lost the vision in that eye, too. When he was ten, he went to the world's first school for the blind and learned to read books with raised letters. But the method used to make the books was expensive and took a lot of labor. As a result, the school had only fourteen books. Louis knew there had to be a better way. When he was just fifteen, he invented Braille writing and spent the rest of his life teaching people who were blind.

Braille is a writing system made up of patterns of raised dots inside cells. A blind person can run his or her finger across the dots and recognize the pattern. He or she can tell what each letter is by using a fingertip. There can be between two and six dots in a single cell; each cell represents a letter, a numeral, or a punctuation mark. Some frequently used words and letter combinations (such as *th*) have their own single-cell patterns.

There are two grades of Braille. In Grade One, a person learns the twenty-six letters of the alphabet and punctuation. To get started with Braille, beginners learn Grade One. In Grade Two, a person knows everything in Grade One plus learns contractions. The contractions conserve space since a Braille page cannot hold as much text as a printed page. All books, menus, public signs, and most Braille materials use Grade Two. Braille is used to write many different languages, including Chinese. Many books are now on CD, allowing blind people to listen to them. However, Braille is still the way that most blind people read and write.

From the time Thomas Gallaudet was born in 1787, he was always smaller and weaker than other kids. He was often left out of their games, and he often felt rejected. He spent a lot of time studying and was so smart that he graduated from Yale University at the age of seventeen. Thomas believed that all people should be included, and no one should feel lonely. He noticed that people often ignored deaf people at social events. They were left out because they could not follow a conversation.

Thomas decided to do something about it. He started the first church and first free school for the deaf in the United States. Someone had already created a manual alphabet to let people represent letters with their fingers. This manual alphabet is still used when a word must be spelled. But Thomas created American Sign Language, which is even more useful. It sped things up because one hand signal means a whole word. When a speaker is talking, an interpreter can keep up. The interpreter can hear. He or she knows sign language and the manual alphabet and can use both to relay the spoken message to a deaf person.

Today, deaf people can use the phone with their computer. First, they call a toll-free number, and then they dial the person to whom they want to talk. A hearing person is the third party in the call. This person types all the words that are spoken, and they appear on the computer screen. It's like the captions you may have seen on DVDs. The deaf person can see the words, and if he or she has any hearing, gets some input from the phone. Some people have been able to use the phone for the first time with this system.

Helping the Blind and Deaf Communicate

Directions: Darken the best answer choice.

1. Braille is used by people who
   Ⓐ cannot walk.
   Ⓑ are deaf.
   Ⓒ cannot move their fingers.
   Ⓓ are blind.

2. An **infection** is a(n)
   Ⓐ illness that can be passed from person to person.
   Ⓑ birth defect.
   Ⓒ serious injury.
   Ⓓ allergy that can kill a person.

3. Which event occurred second?
   Ⓐ Thomas Gallaudet was born.
   Ⓑ Thomas Gallaudet graduated from Yale.
   Ⓒ Louis Braille went blind.
   Ⓓ Louis Braille invented Braille.

4. Which statement is true?
   Ⓐ Thomas Gallaudet invented the manual alphabet.
   Ⓑ There can be up to seven dots in a single Braille cell.
   Ⓒ Multiple spoken languages use Braille as a written language.
   Ⓓ Louis Braille started the first school for the blind.

5. You can infer that
   Ⓐ Louis Braille was deaf as well as blind.
   Ⓑ Thomas Gallaudet was blind.
   Ⓒ It is very difficult to learn Braille or American Sign Language.
   Ⓓ Louis Braille and Thomas Gallaudet changed the world for people with disabilities.

6. One problem with a deaf person using the new phone system with words that appear on the computer screen is that
   Ⓐ the conversation cannot be kept private from the operator.
   Ⓑ the operator may not know how to type.
   Ⓒ most deaf people do not know how to read.
   Ⓓ the operator may not know the language.

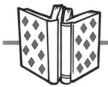

Satellites

A satellite is an object in space. It follows a path, or an orbit. It goes around another thing. Our moon is a satellite. It goes around Earth. Our Earth is a satellite. It goes around the sun. In 1957, the Russians sent up a man-made satellite. It was the first one. Now, more than 5,000 satellites orbit our planet. They do jobs for us. Some take measurements. Others take photos of Earth. Many help communications. They **transmit** signals. These signals let us watch TV. They help us to talk on phones.

How do satellites get up there? They are launched. It takes several rockets to get one into orbit. The first rocket fires. It uses up its fuel. Then, it falls away. The next one fires. It falls away. Each rocket burns up when it hits Earth's atmosphere. It may take three rockets to get the satellite into place. Each satellite must be at an exact height and speed. Why? Its orbit must match the pull of Earth's gravity. This keeps it in the right place.

There are no clouds in space. The sun always shines there. So satellites use solar cells. The solar cells take in the sun's rays. The rays get changed into electric power. The power runs the satellite's equipment. Solar cells can last for years. If they need repair, an astronaut from the space shuttle may fix them.

Not all satellites look alike. But each one has a computer, a communications unit, and a control unit. The computer records data. It stores it, too. The communications unit "talks" to Earth. The control unit carries out commands. People on Earth send the commands.

There are many kinds of satellites. Some watch the oceans and icebergs. They may watch deserts, forests, and animal herds. They may measure air pollution. Spy satellites watch foreign nations. They know where armies and navies are. Weather satellites keep track of clouds. They record wind speeds. This is how forecasters predict our weather. Other satellites keep track of stars and comets. Navigation satellites are up there, too. They let ships and land vehicles know where they are on Earth. Have you seen a GPS unit? It works with three of these satellites. It takes three signals to find a point on Earth.

Communications satellites may be the most important. They orbit high above Earth. They stay right over the equator. They get and send signals. What signals? The ones from TVs and radios. These satellites let us see things as they happen in faraway places. First, trucks with transmitters go to where the news is happening. Someone records the scene with a video camera. Then, it uplinks, or transmits, the sounds and images to a satellite. The satellite gets the information. Then, it downlinks. It sends the signal back to Earth stations. Earth stations, known as satellite dishes, send these signals to your TV set. This process takes just seconds.

In 2009, two communications satellites ran into each other. It was the first time this had ever happened. One was working. But the other one was old. It no longer followed commands. There was no way to make it get out of the way.

Satellites

A satellite is an object in space. It follows a path, or an orbit, around another object. Our moon is a satellite. It goes around Earth. Our Earth is a satellite. It goes around the sun. In 1957, the Russians launched a man-made satellite. It was the first one. Now, more than 5,000 satellites orbit our planet. They do jobs for us. Some take measurements. Others take photos of things happening on Earth. Many help communications. They **transmit** the signals that let us watch TV and talk on phones.

How do satellites get up there? They are launched. It takes several rockets to get one into orbit. The first rocket fires. After it uses up its fuel, it falls away. Then, the next one fires. It falls away. Each rocket burns up as it enters Earth's atmosphere. It may take three rockets to get the satellite into place. Each satellite must be at an exact height and speed. Why? Its orbit must match the pull of Earth's gravity to keep it in place.

There are no clouds in space. The sun always shines there. This lets satellites use solar cells. The solar cells collect the sun's rays. The rays get changed into electric power. The power runs the satellite's equipment. Solar cells can last for years. When they need repair, an astronaut from the space shuttle may fix them.

Not all satellites look the same. But each one has a computer, a communications unit, and a control unit. The computer records and stores data. The communications unit "talks" to Earth. The control unit performs commands. People on Earth send the commands.

There are many kinds of satellites. Astronomical satellites keep track of stars, comets, and meteors. Some satellites watch the oceans and icebergs. They may watch deserts, forests, and animal herds. They may measure air pollution. Spy satellites watch foreign nations. They know where armies and navies are. Weather satellites record clouds and wind speeds. This lets forecasters predict our weather. Navigation satellites let ships and land vehicles know where they are on Earth. A GPS unit works by contacting three of these satellites. It takes three signals to find a point on Earth.

Communications satellites may be the most important. They orbit high above Earth. They stay right over the equator. They broadcast television and radio signals. They let us see events as they happen in faraway places. How? Trucks with transmitters go to where the news is happening. Someone records the scene with a video camera. It uplinks, or transmits, the sounds and images to a satellite. The satellite then downlinks. It sends the signal back to Earth stations. Earth stations, also called satellite dishes, send these signals to your TV set. This whole process takes only a few seconds.

In 2009, two communications satellites ran into each other. It was the first time this had ever happened. One was working, but the other one was old. It no longer followed commands, so there was no way to make it change its course.

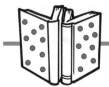

Satellites

A satellite is an object in space that follows a path, or an orbit, around another object. Our moon is a satellite of Earth. Our Earth is a satellite of the sun. In 1957, the Russians launched the first man-made satellite. Now, more than 5,000 of these satellites orbit our planet. They do jobs for us. Some take measurements. Others take photos of things happening on Earth. Many help communications. They **transmit** the signals that let us watch televisions and talk on phones. They let us surf the Internet and get e-mail.

How do satellites get up there? They must be launched. It takes several rockets to boost one into orbit. The first rocket stage fires. After it uses up its fuel, it falls away. Then, the next stage fires and falls away. Each rocket burns up as it enters Earth's atmosphere. It often takes three rockets to get the satellite into place. Why? Each satellite must be put at an exact height and speed. Its orbit must match the pull of Earth's gravity. This holds it in place. Otherwise, it would float off into outer space. The satellites closest to Earth move faster than those farther away.

There are no clouds in space. The sun always shines. This lets satellites run on solar cells. The solar cells collect the sun's rays and change them into electricity to run the satellite's equipment. Solar cells can work for years. When they need repair, an astronaut from the space shuttle may fix them.

Although satellites look different on the outside, they all contain computers, control units, and communications units. The computer records and stores data. The control unit performs commands sent by people on Earth. The communications unit "talks" to Earth.

There are six kinds of satellites. Astronomical satellites keep track of stars, comets, and meteors. Environmental satellites watch the oceans and icebergs. They may watch deserts, forests, and animal herds. They also measure air pollution and holes in the ozone layer. Spy satellites watch foreign nations to keep track of the location of armies and navies. Weather satellites record clouds and wind speeds, which helps forecasters to predict our weather. Navigation satellites let ships and land vehicles know their exact location on Earth. GPS units get their data from these satellites. It takes three signals to locate a point on Earth.

Communications satellites orbit high above Earth. They always stay over the equator. They broadcast television and radio signals. They let us see events as they happen in faraway places. How? Trucks with transmitters go to where the news is happening. Someone records the scene with a video camera. It transmits, or uplinks, the sounds and images to a satellite. The satellite then downlinks. This means that it sends the signal back to Earth stations. Earth stations, also called satellite dishes, send these signals to your television set. The entire process takes just a few seconds!

In 2009, two communications satellites ran into each other. It was the first time this had ever happened. One was working, but the other one was old. It no longer followed commands, so there was no way to make it change its course.

Satellites

Directions: Darken the best answer choice.

1. Once they are orbiting in space, satellites get their electrical power from
   - Ⓐ natural gas.
   - Ⓑ the wind.
   - Ⓒ coal.
   - Ⓓ the sun.

2. The word **transmit** means
   - Ⓐ organize.
   - Ⓑ send.
   - Ⓒ disrupt.
   - Ⓓ reduce.

3. When you watch a news event happening thousands of miles away, which event occurs third?
   - Ⓐ A satellite dish receives a video.
   - Ⓑ Reporters record events using a video camera.
   - Ⓒ A video appears on your TV screen.
   - Ⓓ A video is sent to a satellite orbiting Earth.

4. Which kind of satellite would provide information to help emergency crews predict the path of a wildfire?
   - Ⓐ navigation
   - Ⓑ spy
   - Ⓒ environmental
   - Ⓓ astronomical

5. Complete this analogy: *Moon* is to *Earth* as *satellite* is to
   - Ⓐ *sun.*
   - Ⓑ *satellite dish.*
   - Ⓒ *moon.*
   - Ⓓ *Earth.*

6. You can conclude that
   - Ⓐ satellites collide in space each year.
   - Ⓑ communications satellites have the lowest orbit.
   - Ⓒ satellites are affected by Earth's weather.
   - Ⓓ it costs a lot of money to send a satellite into space.

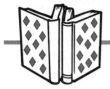

FIRST FLIGHT

FRIDAY, AUGUST 26, 2009

We arrived at J.F.K. International Airport in plenty of time. We checked in our baggage. Then, we walked to the spacious, yet cramped, waiting room. There must have been a million people in that room. I wondered where everyone was going. We had to wait for two hours. It was so boring that it felt like we were waiting for the next leap year to arrive. After what felt like a decade, we finally boarded our plane. We walked out to it on the Jetway®. Basically, the plane parks close to the terminal. The Jetway® is like a movable hallway. It connects the plane with the building. When it's not needed, it folds up like an accordian. I thought that was pretty cool. Plus, there was a lady in a wheelchair. There's no way she could have climbed stairs to get on the plane.

As I waited to take off, I watched a show on the mini TV. It was on the back of the seat in front of me. Everyone had his or her own screen and earphones! I was glad for that TV. It felt like we waited a long time again. Who knew that traveling meant so much waiting?

At last, we started to taxi slowly. We moved out to the runway. First, they shut off the plane's lights and TVs. It was for some safety reason. Then, we started to go faster. I was forced against my seat as the plane picked up speed. We seemed to take off slowly. I looked out the window. We were above New York City. I saw the Brooklyn Bridge, the Manhattan Bridge, the Empire State Building, and the Chrysler Building. Everything in New York City was visible all at once!

About a half hour into our flight, a flight attendant came by. She had chips, cookies, and different sodas. Everyone got to pick something. She let me have a drink and two bags of munchies. I chose pretzels and barbecue corn chips. I watched a comedy show on the TV screen while I enjoyed my snacks.

It was a relaxing flight. It seemed very smooth. The flight attendant said that was because there was no **turbulence**. The noise of the plane's engines didn't bother me. I had thought that it would. But I got used to it right away. I looked at the fluffy, white blanket of clouds below us. The sun was shining. It looked magnificent. Those clouds looked like they would be comfy if you fell asleep on them.

POSTED BY MATT AT 12:34 p.m.   **2 COMMENTS**

Alex said . . .
I wish my first flight was like yours. We had lots of turbulence!
3:40 p.m.

Jake said . . .
The only time I ever flew into J.F.K. it was cloudy, and we couldn't see much of anything.
5:16 p.m.

POST A COMMENT | PREVIOUS POSTS

FIRST FLIGHT

FRIDAY, AUGUST 26, 2009

We arrived at J.F.K. International Airport in plenty of time and checked in our baggage. Then, we walked to the spacious, yet cramped, waiting room. There must have been a million people in that room. I wondered where everyone was going. We had to wait for two hours, but it was so boring that it felt like we were waiting for the next leap year to arrive. After what felt like a decade, we finally boarded our plane. We walked out to it on the Jetway®. Basically, the plane parks close to the terminal, and the Jetway® is like a movable hallway that temporarily connects the plane with the building. When it's not needed, it folds up like an accordian. I thought that was pretty cool. Plus, there was a lady in a wheelchair, and there's no way she could have climbed stairs to get on the plane.

As I waited to take off, I watched a show on the mini TV. It was on the back of the seat in front of me. Everyone had his or her own screen and earphones! I was glad for that TV because it felt like we waited a long time again. Who knew that traveling meant so much waiting?

At last, we started to taxi slowly to the runway. They turned off the plane's lights and TVs for some safety reason. Then, we started to go faster. I was forced against my seat as the plane picked up speed. We seemed to take off slowly. I looked out the window and saw that we were above New York City. I saw the Brooklyn Bridge, the Manhattan Bridge, the Empire State Building, the Chrysler Building—everything in New York City was visible all at once!

About a half hour into our flight, a flight attendant came by and offered chips, cookies, and different sodas. Everyone got to choose something, and she let me have a drink and two bags of munchies. I chose pretzels and barbecue corn chips. I watched a comedy show on the TV screen while I enjoyed my chips and drink.

It was a relaxing flight and very smooth. The flight attendant said there was no **turbulence**. The droning of the plane's engines didn't bother me like I thought it would. I got used to the noise right away. I looked at the fluffy, white blanket of clouds below us. The sun was shining, and it looked magnificent. Those clouds looked like they'd be comfy if you tried to sleep on them.

POSTED BY MATT AT 12:34 p.m.   **2 COMMENTS**

Alex said . . .
I wish my first flight was like yours. We had lots of turbulence!
3:40 p.m.

Jake said . . .
The only time I ever flew into J.F.K. it was cloudy, and we couldn't see much of anything.
5:16 p.m.

POST A COMMENT | PREVIOUS POSTS

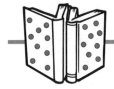

FIRST FLIGHT

FRIDAY, AUGUST 26, 2009

We arrived at J.F.K. International Airport in plenty of time and checked in our baggage before entering the spacious, yet cramped, waiting room. There must have been a million people in that room. I wondered where everyone was going. We had to wait for two hours, but it was so boring that it felt like we were waiting for the next leap year to arrive. After what felt like a decade, we finally boarded our plane by walking on a Jetway®. Basically the plane parks close to the terminal, and the Jetway® is like a movable hallway that temporarily connects the plane with the building. When it's not needed, it folds up like an accordion. I thought that was pretty cool. Plus, there was a lady in a wheelchair, and there's no way she could have climbed stairs to get on the plane.

As I waited to take off, I watched a show on the miniature TV on the back of the seat in front of me. Everyone had his or her own screen and earphones! I was glad for that TV because it felt like we waited a long time again. Who knew that traveling meant so much waiting?

At last, we started to taxi slowly to the runway, and they turned off the plane's lights and TVs for some safety reason. Then, as we started to move faster, I was forced against my seat as the plane picked up speed. We seemed to take off slowly. I looked out the window and saw that we were above New York City. I saw the Brooklyn Bridge, the Manhattan Bridge, the Empire State Building, the Chrysler Building—everything in New York City was visible all at once!

About a half hour into our flight, a flight attendant came by and offered chips, cookies, and different sodas. Everyone got to choose a drink and a snack, and since she let me have two bags of munchies, I chose pretzels and barbecue corn chips. I watched a comedy show on the TV screen while I enjoyed my chips and drink.

It was a relaxing flight and very smooth. The flight attendant said that's because there was no **turbulence**. The droning of the plane's engines didn't bother me like I thought it would; I got used to the noise right away. I looked at the fluffy, white blanket of clouds below us. The sun was shining, and it looked magnificent. Those clouds looked like they would be so comfy if you fell asleep on them.

POSTED BY MATT AT 12:34 p.m.   2 COMMENTS

Alex said . . .
I wish my first flight was like yours. We had lots of turbulence!
3:40 p.m.

Jake said . . .
The only time I ever flew into J.F.K. it was cloudy, and we couldn't see much of anything.
5:16 p.m.

POST A COMMENT | PREVIOUS POSTS

FIRST FLIGHT

Directions: Darken the best answer choice.

1. Two people commented on this blog. They said that they
   Ⓐ had first flights that were a lot like the blogger's.
   Ⓑ had much different experiences when flying.
   Ⓒ had never been on a plane.
   Ⓓ were with the blogger on this trip.

2. The word **turbulence** means
   Ⓐ rough, unpredictable motion.
   Ⓑ malfunction.
   Ⓒ competing for air space.
   Ⓓ confusion.

3. Which event occurred last?
   Ⓐ The blogger walked on a Jetway®.
   Ⓑ The blogger checked in his baggage.
   Ⓒ The blogger waited in a large room for two hours.
   Ⓓ The blogger ate two kinds of snacks.

4. Which of these statements made by the blogger is an exaggeration?
   Ⓐ "There must have been a million people in that room."
   Ⓑ "Everything in New York City was visible all at once!"
   Ⓒ "When it's not needed, it folds up like an accordion."
   Ⓓ "Everyone had his or her own screen and earphones!"

5. Which of these most impressed the blogger?
   Ⓐ the short wait before takeoff
   Ⓑ the way the clouds looked outside the plane
   Ⓒ the noise of the plane's engines
   Ⓓ the lady in the wheelchair not having to climb stairs to board the plane

6. You can tell that the blogger did *not* like
   Ⓐ the snacks he got.
   Ⓑ having his own TV on the plane.
   Ⓒ all the waiting he had to do.
   Ⓓ the amount of turbulence on the flight.

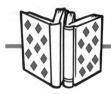

The Wandering Rocks of Death Valley

Death Valley is a desert. It lies in California. It is along Nevada's border. It is the driest place on the North American continent. It is also the lowest and the hottest. Summer temperatures often reach 120°F. Death Valley gets little rain. But when it does, the rain can be heavy. The hard soil cannot absorb a lot of water fast. This can cause flash floods.

Death Valley is an unusual place. Perhaps the oddest part is an area called Racetrack Playa. It is the dry bed of what was once a lake. Racetrack Playa is hard-packed dirt. The hot sun has baked it. It has a rock-like hardness. Rocks are spread all over it. Some are the size of pebbles. Others weigh hundreds of pounds. These rocks slide across the ground.

No one is certain why. There are several theories. One is that night dew makes the ground slick. Another says the dew turns into ice. Both theories say that wind pushes the stones across the mud or ice. Yet the rocks have moved at times when there was no wind. Even when rocks lying next to each other start sliding, one can abruptly change direction. Some of the stones have iron in them. Iron is magnetic. Some scientists have suggested that there may be a magnetic force under the ground. However, that does not seem logical. There have been times when three rocks were close together. Two of them moved in opposite directions. The third one didn't move at all. All agree that the rocks are not sliding downhill. The ground is flat.

During the day, it gets very hot in Death Valley. On average, there are 189 days when the daytime temperature reaches at least 90°F. There are about 138 days when it reaches 100°F! But on many nights, the temperature drops below freezing. Recently, a new theory was put forth. It states that tiny, tiny air pockets inside the rocks shrink. This occurs during the cold nights. Then, during the high heat of day, this air expands. The expanding air pushes on the rocks from the inside. This **propels** the rocks. This could explain why they move in all different directions.

No one has ever seen the rocks move. Nor are there any videos. It is hard to set up time-lapse cameras. There are high winds and flash floods. (During one flash flood, a boulder vanished. It was never found.) However, scientists have kept charts of the stones' positions. At least one of them has moved 659 feet! The rocks leave paths. Some paths are straight. Some loop and twist. Some even go backwards.

An article about these "sliding stones" first appeared in *Life* magazine. It was in 1948. Since then, many people have spent days watching the rocks. They hoped to see one move. Perhaps you will be the first person to see this. If so, you may be the one to solve one of America's oddest mysteries.

The Wandering Rocks of Death Valley

Death Valley is a desert. It lies in California along the border of Nevada. It is the driest, the lowest, and the hottest place on the North American continent. Summer temperatures often reach 120°F. Death Valley gets very little rain. But when it does, the rain may be heavy. The hardened soil cannot absorb a lot of water quickly. This can cause dangerous flash floods.

Death Valley is an unusual place. Perhaps the oddest part is an area called Racetrack Playa. It is the dry bed of what was once a lake. Racetrack Playa is hard-packed earth. The hot sun has baked it to a rock-like hardness. Scattered all over it are rocks. Some are the size of pebbles. Others weigh hundreds of pounds. These rocks mysteriously slide across the ground.

No one is certain why the rocks move. There are several theories. One is that night dew makes the ground slippery. Another says the dew turns into ice. Both theories say that wind pushes the stones across the mud or ice. Yet the rocks have moved at times when there was no wind. And even when rocks lying next to each other start sliding side by side, one can abruptly change direction. Some of the stones contain iron. Iron is magnetic. Scientists have suggested that there may be a magnetic force below the ground. However, that seems illogical. There have been times when three rocks were clustered together. Two of them moved in opposite directions, and the third didn't move at all. All agree that the rocks are not sliding downhill. The ground is flat.

During the day, it gets very hot in Death Valley. On average, there are 189 days when the daytime temperature reaches at least 90°F and 138 days when it reaches 100°F! But on many nights, the temperature drops below freezing. Recently, a new theory was put forth. It states

that tiny, tiny air pockets inside the rocks shrink during the chilly nights. Then, during the intense heat of day, this air expands. The expanding air pushes on the rocks from the inside. This is what **propels** them. This could explain why they move in all different directions.

No one has ever seen the rocks move. Nor are there any videos of the motion. Due to high winds and flash floods, it is hard to set up time-lapse cameras. (During one flash flood, a Racetrack Playa boulder vanished. It was never found.) However, scientists have kept charts of the stones' positions. They know that at least one of them has moved 659 feet! The rocks leave paths. Most tracks are straight. Other tracks loop and twist and even go backwards.

An article about these "sliding stones" first appeared in *Life* magazine in 1948. Since then, countless people have spent days watching the rocks in the hopes of seeing the movement. Perhaps you will be the first fortunate person to witness it. If so, you may be the one to solve one of America's strangest mysteries.

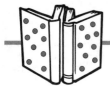
The Wandering Rocks of Death Valley

Death Valley is a desert that lies in California along the border of Nevada. It is the driest, the lowest, and the hottest place on the North American continent. Summer temperatures often reach 120°F. Death Valley gets little rain, but when it does fall, the rain may be heavy. The hardened soil cannot absorb a lot of water quickly, and this can cause dangerous flash floods.

Death Valley is an unusual place. Perhaps the oddest part is an area called Racetrack Playa. It is the dry bed of what was once a lake. Racetrack Playa is hard-packed earth that the hot sun has baked to a rock-like hardness. Scattered all over it are rocks. Some are the size of pebbles; others weigh hundreds of pounds. These rocks mysteriously travel across the ground.

No one is certain why the rocks move. There are several theories. One is that night dew makes the ground slippery. Another says the dew turns into ice. Both theories say that wind pushes the stones across the mud or ice. Yet the rocks have moved at times when there was no wind. And even when rocks lying next to each other start sliding side by side, one can abruptly change direction. Some of the stones contain iron, which is magnetic. Scientists have suggested that there may be a magnetic force below the ground. However, that seems illogical. There have been times when three rocks were clustered together, and two of them moved in opposite directions. The third one didn't move at all. All agree that the rocks are not sliding downhill since the ground is flat.

During the day, it gets very hot in Death Valley. On average, there are 189 days when the daytime temperature reaches at least 90°F and 138 days when it reaches 100°F! But on many nights, the temperature drops below freezing. Recently, a new theory was developed that states that tiny, tiny air pockets inside the rocks shrink during the frosty nights. Then, during the intense heat of day, this air expands. The expanding air pushes on the rocks from the inside and **propels** them. This could explain why they move in all different directions.

No one has ever seen the rocks move. Nor are there any videos of the motion. Due to high winds and flash floods, it is difficult to set up time-lapse cameras. (During one flash flood, a Racetrack Playa boulder vanished and was never found.) However, scientists have kept charts of the stones' positions. At least one of them has moved 659 feet! The rocks leave paths. Most tracks are straight, but other tracks loop and twist and even go backwards.

An article about these "sliding stones" first appeared in *Life* magazine in 1948, and ever since then, countless people have spent days watching the rocks, hoping to spot the movement. Perhaps you will be the first person to witness it. If so, you may be the one to solve one of America's strangest mysteries.

The Wandering Rocks of Death Valley

Directions: Darken the best answer choice.

1. Why are there no videos of the rocks' movement?
   - Ⓐ The desert's heat destroyed the video film in the cameras.
   - Ⓑ No one has ever tried to take videos of the rocks.
   - Ⓒ Scientists do not want to lose their expensive time-lapse cameras to flash floods.
   - Ⓓ Animals knock over the cameras that are set up.

2. The word **propels** means to
   - Ⓐ flip upside down.
   - Ⓑ push.
   - Ⓒ explode.
   - Ⓓ move back and forth rapidly.

3. According to the air pocket theory, what occurs second?
   - Ⓐ The rocks shoot across the ground.
   - Ⓑ Heat makes the air in the pockets of the rocks expand.
   - Ⓒ Tiny air pockets in the rocks shrink during the night.
   - Ⓓ The hot desert sun beats down on the rocks.

4. What is the most unusual fact about Death Valley's environment?
   - Ⓐ the extreme difference between day and night temperatures
   - Ⓑ that desert animals live there
   - Ⓒ that rain rarely falls
   - Ⓓ that high winds sometimes blow

5. Researchers are certain the rocks are *not* being moved by
   - Ⓐ flash floods.
   - Ⓑ strong winds.
   - Ⓒ the force of gravity.
   - Ⓓ magnetic force.

6. People have been watching these rocks, hoping to see them move for more than
   - Ⓐ 60 years.
   - Ⓑ 85 years.
   - Ⓒ 100 years.
   - Ⓓ 200 years.

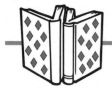

When Booth Saved Lincoln's Life

Robert Todd Lincoln was Abraham Lincoln's oldest son. He was the only one of his four sons to live to adulthood. When Robert grew up, he studied law at Harvard. But he did not graduate. Instead, he joined the Union Army. He worked on Ulysses S. Grant's staff.

During his army service, Robert had an accident. It was on a train platform. It could have killed him. But he was saved from harm. The man who rescued him was Edwin Booth. He was the brother of John Wilkes Booth. This man would soon kill Robert's father.

The event took place in Jersey City, New Jersey. It was in late 1864 or early 1865. (The exact date is not known.) In 1909, Robert Lincoln wrote about his rescue. He sent a letter to the editor of *The Century Magazine*. The magazine printed Robert's account:

"The incident occurred late at night. Passengers were buying their sleeping car places from the conductor. He stood on the station platform at the entrance to the car. The platform was about the height of the car floor. There was a space between the platform and the train car body. There was crowding. I was pressed against the car body. Just then, the train began to move. Its motion twisted me off my feet. I dropped, feet downward, into the open space. I was helpless. Then, my coat collar was **seized**. I was pulled up and out. I got a secure footing on the platform. I turned to thank my rescuer. I saw it was Edwin Booth. His face was well known to me. I expressed my thanks and called him by name."

Edwin Booth was a stage actor. That's why Robert Lincoln knew who he was. Edwin's brother was John Wilkes Booth. He was an actor, too.

In April 1865, John Wilkes Booth shot and killed President Lincoln. A few months later, Robert Lincoln told Colonel Adam Badeau about his rescue. Badeau was friends with Edwin Booth. He praised Booth for saving Robert's life. Edwin had not known the name of the man whom he had saved. When he found out it was the president's son, he was glad. He had been horrified that his brother killed the president.

Do you know of a strange-but-true story? Send it to us at www.realstoriesezine.com

When Booth Saved Lincoln's Life

Robert Todd Lincoln was Abraham Lincoln's oldest son. He was the only one of his four sons to live to adulthood. When Robert grew up, he studied law at Harvard. But he did not graduate. Instead, he joined the Union Army. He worked on Ulysses S. Grant's staff.

During his army service, Robert Lincoln had an accident on a train platform. He was saved from serious harm or even death. The man who rescued him was Edwin T. Booth. He was the brother of John Wilkes Booth, the man who would soon kill Robert's father.

The rescue occurred in Jersey City, New Jersey. It happened in late 1864 or early 1865. (The exact date is unknown.) In 1909, Robert Lincoln wrote about it. He sent a letter to the editor of *The Century Magazine*. The magazine printed Robert's account:

"The incident occurred late at night. Passengers were purchasing their sleeping car places from the conductor. He stood on the station platform at the entrance to the car. The platform was about the height of the car floor. There was a narrow space between the platform and the train car body. There was crowding. I was pressed against the car body while awaiting my turn. Just then, the train began to move. By its motion, I was twisted off my feet. I had dropped, with feet downward, into the open space. I was helpless. Then, my coat collar was **seized**. I was quickly pulled up and out to a secure footing on the platform. Upon turning to thank my rescuer, I saw it was Edwin Booth. His face was well known to me. I expressed my gratitude to him and called him by name."

Edwin Booth was a stage actor. That's why Robert Lincoln knew him instantly. Edwin's brother, John Wilkes Booth, was an actor, too.

In April 1865, John Wilkes Booth shot and killed President Lincoln. A few months later, Robert Lincoln told Colonel Adam Badeau about his near disaster. Badeau was Edwin Booth's friend. He praised Booth for saving Robert Lincoln's life. Edwin had not known the name of the man whom he had saved. When he found out that it was the president's son, he was glad. He had been horrified that his brother killed the president.

Do you know of a strange-but-true story? Send it to us at www.realstoriesezine.com

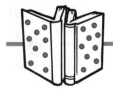

When Booth Saved Lincoln's Life

Robert Todd Lincoln was Abraham Lincoln's oldest son. He was also the only one of his four children to reach adulthood. He studied law at Harvard. But he did not graduate. Instead, he joined the Union Army. He served as a member of Ulysses S. Grant's staff.

During his army service, Robert Lincoln had an accident on a train platform. But he was saved from serious harm, or even death, by Edwin T. Booth. His rescuer was the brother of John Wilkes Booth, the man who would later kill Robert's father.

The rescue occurred in Jersey City, New Jersey, in late 1864 or early 1865. (The exact date has been lost to history.) In 1909, Robert Lincoln sent a letter to the editor of *The Century Magazine* describing what happened. The magazine published Robert's account:

"The incident occurred late at night. Passengers were purchasing their sleeping car places from the conductor. He stood on the station platform at the entrance to the car. The platform was about the height of the car floor. There was a narrow space between the platform and the train car body. There was crowding. I happened to get pressed against the car body while awaiting my turn. Just then, the train began to move. By its motion, I was twisted off my feet. I had dropped somewhat, with feet downward, into the open space. I was helpless. Then, my coat collar was **seized**, and I was quickly pulled up and out to a secure footing on the platform. Upon turning to thank my rescuer, I saw it was Edwin Booth. His face was well known to me. I expressed my gratitude to him and called him by name."

Edwin Booth was a stage actor, and that's why Robert Lincoln instantly recognized him. Edwin's brother, John Wilkes Booth, was an actor, too.

In April 1865, John Wilkes Booth shot and killed President Lincoln in Ford's Theater. A few months later, Robert Lincoln told Colonel Adam Badeau about his near disaster. Badeau, a friend of Edwin Booth's, praised him for saving Robert Lincoln's life. Edwin had not realized that the man he had saved was the president's son. He had been horrified that his brother killed the president, so this knowledge helped him to feel better.

Do you know of a strange-but-true story? Send it to us at www.realstoriesezine.com

The World's Most Mysterious Places

The mysterious places built by those who lived long ago are as amazing as they are **fascinating**. With limited tools, these ancient peoples created splendid works of stone that still stand. We can only wonder why and how they did such things. Open this book and join us on a trip to the world's most mysterious places. See where pharaohs ruled, astronomers watched the skies, and people honored their dead.

Easter Island off the Coast of Chile

Easter Island lies in the South Pacific Ocean. Although the island is small, it is famous. It has many giant human statues. They are hundreds of years old. Those who lived here long ago made them, possibly, to honor dead loved ones. These huge statues were carved by hand. Yet even with today's tools, it would be hard to build one. Some statues have large red rocks sitting atop them. Balancing these stones must have been difficult—and dangerous.

Machu Picchu in Peru

This stone city is at least 600 years old. For years, it lay forgotten high in the Andes Mountains. In 1911, human eyes viewed Machu Picchu once again. In an amazing feat, the stones in the walls fit together perfectly. No mortar was used. Even now, the blade of a knife cannot fit between most of these stones. These people knew that in an area subject to earthquakes, mortar-free construction was sturdier than that which used mortar. So what happened to these people? Why did they leave their city?

Stonehenge in Great Britain

A series of giant stone slabs tower over farm fields. They stand in a set of circles. What was this place? Who built it? And why? The only thing we know for certain about Stonehenge is that it is thousands of years old. The amount of work involved is staggering. Did it act as a calendar, helping the people to identify the summer and winter solstices? Did the people use the stones as a reference point to watch the sun, stars, and moon? Were religious rites held here? Stonehenge is keeping its secrets.

Explore these mysteries and more in *The World's Most Mysterious Places*.

The World's Most Mysterious Places

The mysterious places built by those who lived long ago are as amazing as they are **fascinating**. With limited tools, these ancient peoples created magnificent works of stone that still stand. We can only wonder why and how they did such things. Open this book and join us on a trip to the world's most mysterious places where pharaohs once ruled, astronomers watched the skies, and people honored their dead.

Easter Island off the Coast of Chile

Easter Island lies in the South Pacific Ocean. Although the island is small, it is famous for its many giant human statues that are hundreds of years old. Those who lived here long ago made them, possibly, to honor dead loved ones. These huge statues were carved by hand, yet even with today's tools, it would be hard to build one. Some statues have large red rocks sitting atop them. Balancing these stones must have been difficult—and dangerous.

Machu Picchu in Peru

At least 600 years ago, this city was constructed entirely of stone high in the Andes Mountains. Then, it lay forgotten for years, until 1911, when human eyes saw Machu Picchu once again. In an amazing feat, the stones in the walls fit together so perfectly that no mortar was used. Even now, the blade of a knife cannot fit between most of these stones. These people knew that in a region subject to earthquakes, mortar-free construction was sturdier than that which used mortar. So what happened to these people? Why did they abandon their city?

Stonehenge in Great Britain

A series of giant stone slabs set in circles tower over farm fields. What was this place? Who built it? And why? We can only guess. The only thing we know for certain about Stonehenge is that it is thousands of years old. The amount of work to build it was staggering. Did it act as a calendar, helping the people to identify the summer and winter solstices? Did the people use the stones as a reference point to watch the sun, stars, and moon? Were religious rites held here? Stonehenge is keeping its secrets.

Delve into these mysteries and more in *The World's Most Mysterious Places.*

The World's Most Mysterious Places

Directions: Darken the best answer choice.

1. Machu Picchu was a(n)
   Ⓐ ancient religious rite.
   Ⓑ set of stone slabs.
   Ⓒ specific statue.
   Ⓓ city.

2. The word **fascinating** means
   Ⓐ noticeable.
   Ⓑ confusing.
   Ⓒ unbelievable.
   Ⓓ interesting.

3. Which of these structures is the oldest?
   Ⓐ the statues on Easter Island
   Ⓑ the Statue of Liberty
   Ⓒ Stonehenge
   Ⓓ Machu Picchu

4. All of the places listed on the back of this book
   Ⓐ are thousands of years old.
   Ⓑ were built of stone without modern tools.
   Ⓒ were dangerous to build.
   Ⓓ have been destroyed.

5. What is so amazing about all of these sites?
   Ⓐ Heavy stones were cut and put into place without power equipment.
   Ⓑ Ancient people were willing to die to defend the sites against attackers.
   Ⓒ There's proof that beings from space helped ancient people to construct each site.
   Ⓓ They prove that many ancient people practiced the same religion.

6. Two of the mysterious places are located in
   Ⓐ North America.
   Ⓑ South America.
   Ⓒ Europe.
   Ⓓ Asia.

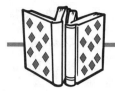

Home   Chinchilla Pictures   Getting to Know Your Chinchilla

Getting to Know Your Chinchilla

A chinchilla is a beautiful rodent. It originally lived wild in the Andes Mountains. It is covered in soft, thick fur. Dogs and cats have been human companions for thousands of years. But the chinchilla has only been **domesticated** for about eighty years. This pet is smart. It has a mind of its own. However, with patient training, a chinchilla can learn to obey. First, it must learn to come out of its cage. Then, you can teach it to come to you when you call its name.

Coming Out of the Cage

When you first get your chinchilla, try to ignore it for a few days. Don't neglect it. But don't try to touch it. Keep the chinchilla's cage in a dark, quiet room. Give it a dark hiding box. When you think that the chinchilla is comfortable with your presence, put your fingers into the cage. Next, feed treats from your fingers. Raisins make the best treats. Cut a raisin into quarters. Only feed four quarters a day. That is one total raisin. More than that is not healthy.

When your chinchilla is comfortable with your hand, put the treats higher up on your arm. It should hop onto your arm by itself. Never force your chinchilla to take a treat. There is another good way to get your chinchilla out of its cage. After it is comfortable with your hand, slip your hand under the chinchilla's belly. Then, lift it up. This prevents escapes out the cage door, too. If at any time your animal is frightened, go back to the previous step. Remember, this takes time. Your chinchilla will not be tamed overnight.

Know this: The worst way to get a chinchilla to come out is to chase it around the cage. This will make your chinchilla fearful. Then it will distrust you. Never chase it! Always wait for your pet to come to you.

Handling Your Chinchilla

Chinchillas like gentle scratches behind the ears and under their chins. Never squeeze the chinchilla's ribs. Its bones are fragile. And never grab your chinchilla by its tail. It can easily break. However, it is safe to hold onto the base of your chinchilla's tail as it sits in your lap or on your arm. The base is where the tail attaches to the body. If you are outdoors and fear your chinchilla might escape, keep a firm grip on the base of its tail.

Never set your pet down outside. This is true even in a fenced yard. Chinchillas are smaller than they look. They can slip through the holes in a chain-link fence. They will find the one crack in the boards of a wooden fence. If your chinchilla gets loose outside, do not chase it. That may cause it to run into the street or hide somewhere (such as under a shed). The best thing you can do is put its cage outside. Leave the door open. Most chinchillas love their cages. It is where they feel safe. It will go back to its cage on its own.

Visitor Number: **0032593**   Last Site Update: **3/11/10**

Contact Us | Chinchilla F.A.Q. | Links

Home   Chinchilla Pictures   Getting to Know Your Chinchilla

Getting to Know Your Chinchilla

A chinchilla is a beautiful rodent originally from the Andes Mountains. It is covered in soft, thick fur. Unlike dogs and cats, which have been human companions for thousands of years, the chinchilla has only been **domesticated** for about eighty years. It is smart and has a strong will. However, with patient training, a chinchilla can learn to come out of its cage and respond to its name.

Coming Out of the Cage

When you first get your chinchilla, try to ignore it for the first few days. Don't neglect it. But don't try to touch it. Keep the chinchilla's cage in a dark, quiet room with a dark hiding box. When you think that the chinchilla is comfortable with your presence, try putting your fingers into the cage. Next, feed treats from your fingers. The best treats are raisins. To make the raisins last, cut them into quarters. Only feed it one total raisin a day. More than that is not healthy.

When your chinchilla is comfortable with your hand, put treats higher up on your arm. The pet should hop right onto your arm. Never force your chinchilla to take its treat. Another good way to get your chinchilla out of its cage is to let it get comfortable with your hand so that you can slip your hand under its belly and lift it up. This prevents escaping out the cage door, too. If at any time your animal is uncomfortable, go back to the previous step. Remember, this takes time. Your chinchilla will not become tame overnight.

Know this: The worst way to get a chinchilla to come out is to chase it around the cage. This will make your chinchilla fearful. Then it will distrust you. Never chase it! Always wait for your pet to come to you.

Handling Your Chinchilla

Chinchillas like gentle scratches behind the ears and under their chins. Never squeeze the chinchilla's rib area. Its bones are fragile. And never grab your chinchilla by its tail. You can easily break it. However, it is safe to hold onto the base of your chinchilla's tail while it sits in your lap or on your arm. The base is where the tail attaches to the body. If you are outdoors and afraid your chinchilla might escape, be sure you have a firm grip on the base of its tail.

Never set your pet down outside. This is true even in a fenced yard. Chinchillas are much smaller than they look. They can easily slip through the holes in a chain-link fence. They will find the one crack in the boards of your wooden fence. If your chinchilla gets loose outside, do not chase it. That may cause your chinchilla to run into the street or hide somewhere you cannot reach (such as under a shed). The best thing you can do is put its cage outside with the door open. Most chinchillas love their cages. It is where they feel safe. It will return to its cage on its own.

Visitor Number: **0032593**   Last Site Update: **3/11/10**

Contact Us | Chinchilla F.A.Q. | Links

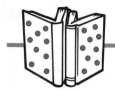

Home   **Chinchilla Pictures**   Getting to Know Your Chinchilla

Getting to Know Your Chinchilla

Originally from the Andes Mountains, a chinchilla is a beautiful rodent covered in soft, thick fur. Unlike dogs and cats, which have been human companions for thousands of years, the chinchilla has only been **domesticated** for about eighty years. It is smart and has a strong will. However, with patient training, a chinchilla can learn to come out of its cage and respond to its name.

Coming Out of the Cage

When you first get your chinchilla, try to ignore it for the first few days. Don't neglect it, but don't try to touch it. Keep the chinchilla's cage in a dark, quiet room with a dark hiding box. When you sense that the chinchilla is comfortable with your presence, try putting your fingers into the cage. Next, feed treats from your fingers. The best treats are raisins. To make the raisins last, cut them into quarters. Only feed it one total raisin a day, since more than that is not healthy.

When your chinchilla is comfortable with your hand, put treats higher up on your arm, and it should hop right onto your arm. Never force your chinchilla to take its treat. Another good way to get your chinchilla out of its cage is to let it get comfortable with your hand so that you can slip your hand under its belly and lift it up. This prevents escaping out the cage door, too. If at any time your animal seems uncomfortable, go back to the previous step. Be patient and remember, this takes time. Your chinchilla will not become tame overnight.

Know this: The worst way to get a chinchilla to come out is to chase it around the cage. This will make your chinchilla fearful, and then it will distrust you. Never chase it! Always wait for your pet to come to you.

Handling Your Chinchilla

Chinchillas like gentle scratches behind the ears and under their chins. Never squeeze the chinchilla's rib area because its bones are fragile. And never grab your chinchilla by its tail, which can easily break. However, you can grasp the base of your chinchilla's tail (where it attaches to the body) while it sits in your lap or on your arm. If you are outdoors and afraid your chinchilla might escape, be sure you have a firm grip on the base of its tail.

Never set your pet down outside, even in a fenced yard. Chinchillas are much smaller than they look and can easily slip through the holes in a chain-link fence. They will find the one crack in the boards of your wooden fence. If your chinchilla gets loose outside, do not chase it. That may cause your chinchilla to run into the street or hide somewhere you cannot reach (such as under a shed). The best thing you can do is put its cage outside with the door open. Most chinchillas love their cages since it is where they feel safe. It will return to its cage by itself.

Visitor Number: 0032593   **Last Site Update: 3/11/10**

Contact Us | Chinchilla F.A.Q. | Links

Web Site

Getting to Know Your Chinchilla

Directions: Darken the best answer choice.

1. The best way to pick up a chinchilla is to
    Ⓐ pinch both ears together and lift up.
    Ⓑ grab it by the base of its tail.
    Ⓒ slide your hand beneath its belly.
    Ⓓ grasp it firmly around the middle.

2. The word **domesticated** means
    Ⓐ tamed.
    Ⓑ identified.
    Ⓒ available.
    Ⓓ discovered.

3. When teaching your chinchilla to come out of its cage to you, which of these is the last step?
    Ⓐ Put the chinchilla's cage in a quiet room.
    Ⓑ Put pieces of raisins on your arm.
    Ⓒ Put your hand inside the cage.
    Ⓓ Don't try to touch the chinchilla for a few days.

4. Compared to a dog, a chinchilla will probably
    Ⓐ trust its new owner immediately.
    Ⓑ make alot more noise.
    Ⓒ need more space.
    Ⓓ enjoy its cage.

5. Chinchillas
    Ⓐ need time and patience in order to trust their owners.
    Ⓑ can run around safely in a fenced yard.
    Ⓒ often bite their owners.
    Ⓓ like bright rooms.

6. Why do chinchillas act more wild than cats?
    Ⓐ Chinchillas are taken from the wild and brought to your pet store.
    Ⓑ Chinchillas have not been kept as pets as long as cats have.
    Ⓒ Chinchillas do not like humans and can be stubborn.
    Ⓓ Chinchillas must roam around outdoors to find their own food.

Answer Sheet

Name: _____

Title: _____

Page: _____

1. Ⓐ   Ⓑ   Ⓒ   Ⓓ
2. Ⓐ   Ⓑ   Ⓒ   Ⓓ
3. Ⓐ   Ⓑ   Ⓒ   Ⓓ
4. Ⓐ   Ⓑ   Ⓒ   Ⓓ
5. Ⓐ   Ⓑ   Ⓒ   Ⓓ
6. Ⓐ   Ⓑ   Ⓒ   Ⓓ

Answer Sheet

Name: _____

Title: _____

Page: _____

1. Ⓐ   Ⓑ   Ⓒ   Ⓓ
2. Ⓐ   Ⓑ   Ⓒ   Ⓓ
3. Ⓐ   Ⓑ   Ⓒ   Ⓓ
4. Ⓐ   Ⓑ   Ⓒ   Ⓓ
5. Ⓐ   Ⓑ   Ⓒ   Ⓓ
6. Ⓐ   Ⓑ   Ⓒ   Ⓓ

Answer Sheet

Name: _____

Title: _____

Page: _____

1. Ⓐ   Ⓑ   Ⓒ   Ⓓ
2. Ⓐ   Ⓑ   Ⓒ   Ⓓ
3. Ⓐ   Ⓑ   Ⓒ   Ⓓ
4. Ⓐ   Ⓑ   Ⓒ   Ⓓ
5. Ⓐ   Ⓑ   Ⓒ   Ⓓ
6. Ⓐ   Ⓑ   Ⓒ   Ⓓ

Answer Sheet

Name: _____

Title: _____

Page: _____

1. Ⓐ   Ⓑ   Ⓒ   Ⓓ
2. Ⓐ   Ⓑ   Ⓒ   Ⓓ
3. Ⓐ   Ⓑ   Ⓒ   Ⓓ
4. Ⓐ   Ⓑ   Ⓒ   Ⓓ
5. Ⓐ   Ⓑ   Ⓒ   Ⓓ
6. Ⓐ   Ⓑ   Ⓒ   Ⓓ

Answer Sheet

Name: _____

page 17
1. Ⓐ Ⓑ Ⓒ Ⓓ
2. Ⓐ Ⓑ Ⓒ Ⓓ
3. Ⓐ Ⓑ Ⓒ Ⓓ
4. Ⓐ Ⓑ Ⓒ Ⓓ
5. Ⓐ Ⓑ Ⓒ Ⓓ
6. Ⓐ Ⓑ Ⓒ Ⓓ

page 37
1. Ⓐ Ⓑ Ⓒ Ⓓ
2. Ⓐ Ⓑ Ⓒ Ⓓ
3. Ⓐ Ⓑ Ⓒ Ⓓ
4. Ⓐ Ⓑ Ⓒ Ⓓ
5. Ⓐ Ⓑ Ⓒ Ⓓ
6. Ⓐ Ⓑ Ⓒ Ⓓ

page 57
1. Ⓐ Ⓑ Ⓒ Ⓓ
2. Ⓐ Ⓑ Ⓒ Ⓓ
3. Ⓐ Ⓑ Ⓒ Ⓓ
4. Ⓐ Ⓑ Ⓒ Ⓓ
5. Ⓐ Ⓑ Ⓒ Ⓓ
6. Ⓐ Ⓑ Ⓒ Ⓓ

page 77
1. Ⓐ Ⓑ Ⓒ Ⓓ
2. Ⓐ Ⓑ Ⓒ Ⓓ
3. Ⓐ Ⓑ Ⓒ Ⓓ
4. Ⓐ Ⓑ Ⓒ Ⓓ
5. Ⓐ Ⓑ Ⓒ Ⓓ
6. Ⓐ Ⓑ Ⓒ Ⓓ

page 21
1. Ⓐ Ⓑ Ⓒ Ⓓ
2. Ⓐ Ⓑ Ⓒ Ⓓ
3. Ⓐ Ⓑ Ⓒ Ⓓ
4. Ⓐ Ⓑ Ⓒ Ⓓ
5. Ⓐ Ⓑ Ⓒ Ⓓ
6. Ⓐ Ⓑ Ⓒ Ⓓ

page 41
1. Ⓐ Ⓑ Ⓒ Ⓓ
2. Ⓐ Ⓑ Ⓒ Ⓓ
3. Ⓐ Ⓑ Ⓒ Ⓓ
4. Ⓐ Ⓑ Ⓒ Ⓓ
5. Ⓐ Ⓑ Ⓒ Ⓓ
6. Ⓐ Ⓑ Ⓒ Ⓓ

page 61
1. Ⓐ Ⓑ Ⓒ Ⓓ
2. Ⓐ Ⓑ Ⓒ Ⓓ
3. Ⓐ Ⓑ Ⓒ Ⓓ
4. Ⓐ Ⓑ Ⓒ Ⓓ
5. Ⓐ Ⓑ Ⓒ Ⓓ
6. Ⓐ Ⓑ Ⓒ Ⓓ

page 81
1. Ⓐ Ⓑ Ⓒ Ⓓ
2. Ⓐ Ⓑ Ⓒ Ⓓ
3. Ⓐ Ⓑ Ⓒ Ⓓ
4. Ⓐ Ⓑ Ⓒ Ⓓ
5. Ⓐ Ⓑ Ⓒ Ⓓ
6. Ⓐ Ⓑ Ⓒ Ⓓ

page 25
1. Ⓐ Ⓑ Ⓒ Ⓓ
2. Ⓐ Ⓑ Ⓒ Ⓓ
3. Ⓐ Ⓑ Ⓒ Ⓓ
4. Ⓐ Ⓑ Ⓒ Ⓓ
5. Ⓐ Ⓑ Ⓒ Ⓓ
6. Ⓐ Ⓑ Ⓒ Ⓓ

page 45
1. Ⓐ Ⓑ Ⓒ Ⓓ
2. Ⓐ Ⓑ Ⓒ Ⓓ
3. Ⓐ Ⓑ Ⓒ Ⓓ
4. Ⓐ Ⓑ Ⓒ Ⓓ
5. Ⓐ Ⓑ Ⓒ Ⓓ
6. Ⓐ Ⓑ Ⓒ Ⓓ

page 65
1. Ⓐ Ⓑ Ⓒ Ⓓ
2. Ⓐ Ⓑ Ⓒ Ⓓ
3. Ⓐ Ⓑ Ⓒ Ⓓ
4. Ⓐ Ⓑ Ⓒ Ⓓ
5. Ⓐ Ⓑ Ⓒ Ⓓ
6. Ⓐ Ⓑ Ⓒ Ⓓ

page 85
1. Ⓐ Ⓑ Ⓒ Ⓓ
2. Ⓐ Ⓑ Ⓒ Ⓓ
3. Ⓐ Ⓑ Ⓒ Ⓓ
4. Ⓐ Ⓑ Ⓒ Ⓓ
5. Ⓐ Ⓑ Ⓒ Ⓓ
6. Ⓐ Ⓑ Ⓒ Ⓓ

page 29
1. Ⓐ Ⓑ Ⓒ Ⓓ
2. Ⓐ Ⓑ Ⓒ Ⓓ
3. Ⓐ Ⓑ Ⓒ Ⓓ
4. Ⓐ Ⓑ Ⓒ Ⓓ
5. Ⓐ Ⓑ Ⓒ Ⓓ
6. Ⓐ Ⓑ Ⓒ Ⓓ

page 49
1. Ⓐ Ⓑ Ⓒ Ⓓ
2. Ⓐ Ⓑ Ⓒ Ⓓ
3. Ⓐ Ⓑ Ⓒ Ⓓ
4. Ⓐ Ⓑ Ⓒ Ⓓ
5. Ⓐ Ⓑ Ⓒ Ⓓ
6. Ⓐ Ⓑ Ⓒ Ⓓ

page 69
1. Ⓐ Ⓑ Ⓒ Ⓓ
2. Ⓐ Ⓑ Ⓒ Ⓓ
3. Ⓐ Ⓑ Ⓒ Ⓓ
4. Ⓐ Ⓑ Ⓒ Ⓓ
5. Ⓐ Ⓑ Ⓒ Ⓓ
6. Ⓐ Ⓑ Ⓒ Ⓓ

page 89
1. Ⓐ Ⓑ Ⓒ Ⓓ
2. Ⓐ Ⓑ Ⓒ Ⓓ
3. Ⓐ Ⓑ Ⓒ Ⓓ
4. Ⓐ Ⓑ Ⓒ Ⓓ
5. Ⓐ Ⓑ Ⓒ Ⓓ
6. Ⓐ Ⓑ Ⓒ Ⓓ

page 33
1. Ⓐ Ⓑ Ⓒ Ⓓ
2. Ⓐ Ⓑ Ⓒ Ⓓ
3. Ⓐ Ⓑ Ⓒ Ⓓ
4. Ⓐ Ⓑ Ⓒ Ⓓ
5. Ⓐ Ⓑ Ⓒ Ⓓ
6. Ⓐ Ⓑ Ⓒ Ⓓ

page 53
1. Ⓐ Ⓑ Ⓒ Ⓓ
2. Ⓐ Ⓑ Ⓒ Ⓓ
3. Ⓐ Ⓑ Ⓒ Ⓓ
4. Ⓐ Ⓑ Ⓒ Ⓓ
5. Ⓐ Ⓑ Ⓒ Ⓓ
6. Ⓐ Ⓑ Ⓒ Ⓓ

page 73
1. Ⓐ Ⓑ Ⓒ Ⓓ
2. Ⓐ Ⓑ Ⓒ Ⓓ
3. Ⓐ Ⓑ Ⓒ Ⓓ
4. Ⓐ Ⓑ Ⓒ Ⓓ
5. Ⓐ Ⓑ Ⓒ Ⓓ
6. Ⓐ Ⓑ Ⓒ Ⓓ

page 93
1. Ⓐ Ⓑ Ⓒ Ⓓ
2. Ⓐ Ⓑ Ⓒ Ⓓ
3. Ⓐ Ⓑ Ⓒ Ⓓ
4. Ⓐ Ⓑ Ⓒ Ⓓ
5. Ⓐ Ⓑ Ⓒ Ⓓ
6. Ⓐ Ⓑ Ⓒ Ⓓ

Answer Key

page 17
1. B
2. A
3. C
4. D
5. B
6. D

page 21
1. A
2. B
3. C
4. C
5. A
6. B

page 25
1. C
2. A
3. D
4. B
5. C
6. B

page 29
1. D
2. C
3. B
4. A
5. D
6. B

page 33
1. C
2. D
3. A
4. B
5. C
6. A

page 37
1. B
2. D
3. C
4. C
5. B
6. A

page 41
1. C
2. C
3. D
4. A
5. B
6. A

page 45
1. D
2. A
3. B
4. D
5. B
6. C

page 49
1. B
2. D
3. B
4. C
5. A
6. A

page 53
1. B
2. C
3. D
4. B
5. D
6. A

page 57
1. A
2. D
3. C
4. B
5. A
6. C

page 61
1. C
2. B
3. A
4. C
5. D
6. B

page 65
1. A
2. D
3. B
4. C
5. A
6. B

page 69
1. D
2. A
3. B
4. C
5. D
6. A

page 73
1. D
2. B
3. A
4. C
5. D
6. D

page 77
1. B
2. A
3. D
4. A
5. B
6. C

page 81
1. C
2. B
3. D
4. A
5. C
6. A

page 85
1. D
2. C
3. B
4. A
5. C
6. D

page 89
1. D
2. D
3. C
4. B
5. A
6. B

page 93
1. C
2. A
3. B
4. D
5. A
6. B